VOICES
FROM THE
WHIRLWIND

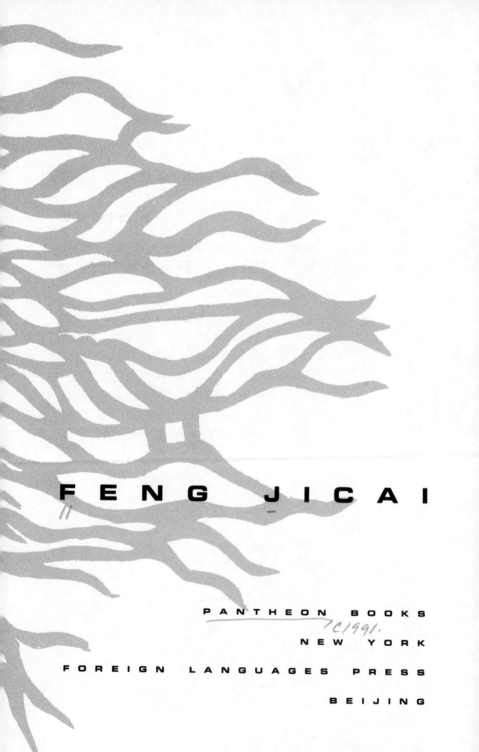

FENG JICAI

PANTHEON BOOKS

NEW YORK

FOREIGN LANGUAGES PRESS

BEIJING

" VOICES

FROM THE

WHIRLWIND. "

An Oral History of the

Chinese Cultural Revolution

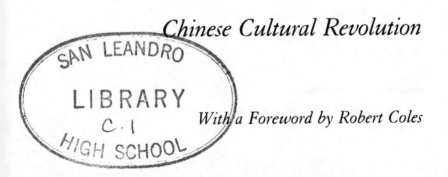

With a Foreword by Robert Coles

Library of Congress Cataloging-in-Publication Data
Feng, Chi-ts'ai.
    [I pai ko jen ti shih nien. English. Selections]
    Voices from the whirlwind: an oral history of the Chinese cultural
revolution / by Feng Jicai; foreword by Robert Coles.
        p.   cm.
    A collection of 14 first-person accounts selected and translated from:
I pai ko jen ti shih nien.
    Includes index.
    ISBN 0-394-58645-X
    1. China—History—Cultural Revolution, 1966–1969—Personal
narratives.   I. Title.
DS778.7.F462513   1991
951.05'6—dc20
                                                                90-52565

Book design by Chris Welch
Manufactured in the United States of America
First Edition

CONTENTS

CONTENTS

What follows are heart-breaking, yet ever so instructive decla-rations, memories, avowals; narrative presentations of life as it was lived in a great nation going through a terrible moral and political crisis. What follows, too, is history as it can be evoked and portrayed from the bottom up, so to speak—not the history of big-shot politicians and generals, not the history of historians either, but rather the history of ordinary men and women who suddenly, out of nowhere it seemed, did indeed feel the anxiety and pain, the continual terror that arrived in the name of a "Cultural Revolution;" a "whirlwind" for sure; so much swept away, so much shaken and buffeted, tossed about and torn apart.

As one reads these remembrances, one yet again realizes that our lives are not given shape only by the early childhood we happen to live, or even the particular social and economic world we inherit from our parents and grandparents. A nation's ups and downs, its political history, can become the ruling force upon the lives of thousands, millions of men, women, children —and, in some cases, can become instruments of terror and genocide. Because a "Cultural Revolution" took place, all sorts of human beings joined the ranks of the insulted and the injured, the scorned and the rebuked, their lives significantly changed—in some cases irreparably changed, and alas, in some cases, ended.

Those who speak in the pages that follow survived, though with minds that surely struggle hard, day and night, to put aside one central evil: what leaders who abuse power can do to their own people in the name of ideology. Here was a nightmare not unique to any country or continent; here was meanness and abusiveness become a national craziness: hysterical and cruel accusations and intimidations, lies and more lies, rumors turned into the clubs of vilification and even murder. Whole families, we get to know, were wrongfully arraigned or hunted down, and often enough, convicted of imaginary crimes, victims of a spell of out-and-out political madness that got turned into the everyday, wanton persecution of the innocent by the all too self-serving and self-aggrandizing—a nation's scandal and its shame.

Yet, amid such awful circumstances, amid so much wrongdoing and evil, amid a kind of panic and wickedness of vast proportions, and for a while, of seemingly endless duration, any number of vulnerable men and women and children managed to survive—not only survive in body, but in mind and soul. The "Cultural Revolution" was at heart a crazed, wanton assault on one part of a country's people by another part—an effort of some to frighten and intimidate others, to drive them into a land of fear and trembling, to use accusation in hopes that endless self-accusation would follow. The blind attempted to blind others (ideology run amok results in a loss of vision, a descent into the hell of slogans, clichés, rituals, rote exercises in surrender to anyone and everyone). Still, some kept their vision, saw clearly the lunatic excesses of their countrymen, whether in

---

high or low places, and kept their eyes on what mattered, on a future they could only hope would come sooner rather than later. These "oral histories" are testimony to that kind of visionary survival: a moral and psychological triumph of enormous significance.

As I read these personal stories, each with its own losses and hurts to report, its own endurance and courage and resourcefulness to chronicle, I realized what totalitarianism can come to mean in the life of a nation, a people: the loss of all respect for the personal dignity of the individual; the constant hectoring through state-owned radio and television; the use of rumor, innuendo, gossip, and lies of all sorts as a means of scaring people, destroying their sense of their worth, their rights as human beings; and finally, the hounding of those people, the arrests and arraignments, the threats and beatings and denunciations and jailings.

Here is the social and political reality that writers such as Kafka only imagined: stories of a world gone cruelly wild; but stories, too, of resiliency, of endurance, of extraordinary courage demonstrated against the worst odds imaginable. We are lucky to know the people who appear in this book; their stories have much to teach us, not only about them, but about us; their unlucky fate and our enormous good fortune to be spared, so far, such a fate.

—Robert Coles
Cambridge, Massachusetts
1990

KEY FIGURES DURING THE CULTURAL REVOLUTION

CHEN YUN   Member of the Standing Committee of the Communist Party (CCP) Politburo (1956–1966); Vice-Chairman of the Central Committee of the CCP (1978).

DENG XIAOPING   Secretary General of the CCP (1956–1966); Vice-Premier of the State Council (1973); Vice-Chairman of the Central Committee (1975, 1977).

THE GANG OF FOUR   **Jiang Qing,** the wife of Mao Zedong and Politburo member (1973–1976); **Wang Hongwen,** former textile mill worker who became Vice-Chairman of the CCP in 1973; **Yao Wenyuan,** editor at the Shanghai *Liberation Daily,* who became a Politburo member in 1973; and **Zhang Qunqiao,** secretary of CCP Shanghai Municipal Committee who became a Politburo member in 1973, then Vice-Premier of the State Council in 1975.

LIN BIAO   Vice-Chairman of the Military Commission of the Central Committee of the CCP, and minister of defense (1959–1971).

LIU SHAOQI   Chairman of the People's Republic of China (1959–1966).

MAO ZEDONG   Chairman of the Central Committee of the CCP.

PENG ZHEN   Mayor of Beijing.

ZHOU ENLAI   Premier of the State Council.

1957
February–April: Mao Zedong advocates rapprochement with non-Party intellectuals and invites them to criticize the "bureaucracy, sectarianism, and subjectivism" plaguing the CCP.

May–June: In the face of strident criticism and challenges to the CCP's authority by intellectuals, Mao and the Central Committee call for a crackdown, resulting in the "Antirightist" movement.

Winter: The "Antirightist" movement climaxes when more than 550,000 intellectuals are labeled "Rightists"; many are forced to leave their positions in the cities to work on farms in the country.

1958
August: The Great Leap Forward. The CCP initiates a plan to increase the nation's industrial and agricultural production by abolishing private plots and organizing people's communes throughout rural China.

1959–1962

Agricultural production falls short of exaggerated estimates, and a nationwide famine hits China. An estimated 30 million people die of famine-related causes.

1965

November: In a newspaper article generally regarded as the spark that sets off the Cultural Revolution, Yao Wenyuan criticizes *The Dismissal of Hai Rui from Office,* a play by Wu Han, vice-mayor of Beijing. Despite Mao's endorsement of Yao's essay, Beijing newspapers decline to publish it.

1966

The Cultural Revolution begins. Mao decries the bureaucratization and stagnation in the CCP, blaming officials who are taking the "capitalist road." Lin Biao, in an attempt to improve his own position in the CCP hierarchy, incites blind idolization of Mao among the people.

June 1: An editorial, "Sweep Away All Monsters," appears in *The People's Daily,* urging people to purge bourgeois ideology from the cultural sphere. Beijing's mayor, Peng Zhen, is ousted, along with Luo Ruiqing, vice-premier and Army chief of staff; Lu Dingyi, Politburo member and director of propaganda; and Yang Shangkun, member of the Central Committee.

August 8: The Party Central Committee issues a sixteen-point directive calling on the people to guard against counter-revolutionary subversion. The Red Guards—radical students devoted to Mao—are organized to safeguard the revolution, resulting in widespread violence. Intellectuals are persecuted and tortured; some commit suicide. Millions are sent to rural areas to be reformed through labor.

Lin Biao is designated Mao's heir apparent.

1967

January: "The January Storm." Rebels in Shanghai seize power from Party organs. Red Guard organizations throughout China follow suit, ousting Party and government officials. A New Year's Day editorial in *The People's Daily* calls for a coalition of workers and peasants to overthrow the heads of factories, mines, and rural areas. In the ensuing months, revolutionary committees are established, replacing Party committees and government agencies at all levels.

The CCP Central Committee, Military Committee, and State Council call on the People's Liberation Army (PLA) to support "Left workers and peasants," and institute military control and training.

Summer: The PLA is ordered to disband all "counterrevolutionary organizations." Scores of civilians and soldiers are killed.

1968

December 22: *The People's Daily* publishes Mao's directive for educated young people to "go to the countryside" for reeducation by "the poor and lower-middle peasants." Thousands of students respond to the call.

1968–1969

According to Mao's directive of 7 May 1968, farm schools—the May Seventh Cadre Schools—are established throughout the country, where Red Guard cadres, government officials, as well as suspected "bad elements" are sent for ideological reeducation through manual labor. Liu Shaoqi, the deposed chairman of the People's Republic, is among those sent away. He dies in prison in 1969.

1971

September 13: Suspected of plotting an attempt on Mao's life, Lin Biao flees China with his wife and son. All three are reportedly killed in an airplane crash in Mongolia.

1972

February: Richard Nixon visits China, signaling the beginning of normalized Sino–U.S. relations.

1976

January 8: Premier Zhou Enlai dies.

April 5: During the Qingming Festival (a memorial festival for the dead) in Tiananmen Square, spontaneous mass demonstrations honoring the memory of Zhou Enlai and denouncing the Gang of Four are violently suppressed.

April 7: The Tiananmen Square incident is declared "a counterrevolutionary political incident." Deng Xiaoping is denounced as the instigator and stripped of power.

September 9: Mao Zedong dies.

October 6: The Gang of Four is arrested, marking the end of the Cultural Revolution.

December 5: Those persecuted for their opposition to the Gang of Four are declared "rehabilitated" by the CCP Central Committee.

Voices

From the

Whirlwind

THEY
WHO HAVE
SUFFERED
GREATLY

TIME: *1969* 🦋 AGE: *17* 🦋 SEX: *Male*
OCCUPATION: *Deputy company commander of a state farm in H Province*[1]

'm thirty-four years old. I was fourteen when the Cultural Revolution began and twenty-four when it ended. You're probably thinking I'm not like the people whose hair had turned completely gray by the end of the Cultural Revolution, or the ones who, even though they were just past fifty, had lost the best years of their lives and just threw in the towel. I seem to be doing OK, right? But even if I live to be seventy, I'll still feel I packed a whole lifetime's worth of living into those ten years.

If I told you everything, it would take days, so I'll give you a very condensed account, OK?

I'll focus on my experience in Heilongjiang.[2] Before then I was in school, and though I had plenty of thoughts and feelings there, they were nothing compared to the ones I had in Heilongjiang, out in the real world. I like literature because it's taught me how to understand myself and others, and informed me about society and life. But I hate literature too, because it makes me understand things too well, and that makes my mental burden even heavier.

I often wonder why going down to the countryside back then means so much to me and my generation. It wasn't just the physical labor, it was the way our fates became tied up with society, politics, economics, and culture during the Going to the Countryside Movement,[3] all set against the specific historical background of the Cultural Revolution. While each of us went through completely different experiences, each of us also represents the process of growing up in that time. Is it OK to say that? It's not overstating things, right? That's my feeling, anyway.

I was class of '68. The Cultural Revolution came in my first year of junior high school. You could say I knew what was what then, and you could also say I didn't know a thing. I was born into an ordinary workers' family. My father got TB before Liberation[4] and was going to die, and the boss fired him. Fortunately, Liberation came, and the state paid to send him to the hospital and cure him. It's no lie to say that the new society gave him a new lease on life. My mother's family was relatively well-off. Her first husband had gotten sick and died. After Liberation my father and mother both worked in a tailoring cooperative run by the neighborhood committee. My father could read, and taught classes. My mother taught tailoring to women just starting to work outside the home. They fell in love. My mother's brother was a capitalist who violently opposed my mother's second marriage because my father was poor. She followed her heart and married him anyway. First they had me, then my little sister. Our lives were hard. My uncle lived in a house with a courtyard just north of us. Whenever my mother went over, they were always on guard, in case she was coming to borrow money. In all those years, they never helped us out once. Whenever we kids went there to play, they always thought we were going to steal something because we were poor, and managed to find an excuse to get rid of us.

When the Cultural Revolution started, my uncle the capitalist was a "monster,"[5] of course, and his house was ransacked and all his property taken away. Life was hard for him, since he was used to living comfortably. Every month my mother managed to scrape together some money to give them. Though I was young at the time, I had a deep understanding of life. Nowadays you'd say I knew the way things were. That's why I had great respect for my parents. They were honest and kind people.

Considering my circumstances, would you think I'd have any problems loving the Party, the new society, or Chairman Mao? But it wasn't nearly that simple. When the Cultural Revolution began, all the students wanted to join the Red Guards.[6] However, it seemed there was a problem with my grandfather. What was it? Before Liberation, he had been a tax collector in a small town in Yunnan. When he and his boss were on their way to the provincial capital on business he was shot in the leg by some arms smugglers and bled to death. After Liberation, in response to my father's application to join the Party, they went to my grandfather's mother to investigate the situation. The old lady still thought in the old way and, because she was afraid people would look down on our family for being poor, she said, "My son made hundreds of yuan a month, he was a bureau chief there, rolling in money!" The Party man didn't believe her and said, "If your son made so much money, then, before Liberation, why did your grandson [my father] get so sick he almost died?" The old lady couldn't answer. So there was no way to settle my grandfather's status and the Party didn't have the money to go down to Yunnan and conduct an investigation on behalf of an ordinary guy like my dad, so the case was never resolved. And it continued to have an impact right up to my joining the Red Guards and the Party.

Looking back now, you'll think it's funny. But at the time I could only join the Mao Zedong Thought Outer Red Guards. At that time, Red Guards were divided into three classes. First-class citizens, the children of high-ranking cadres,[7] became Maoist Red Guards. Second-class citizens, the children of workers or poor and lower middle-class peasants, became Mao Zedong Thought Red Guards. The third group was made up of those who weren't from the five black categories[8] but weren't very pure either: They joined the Mao Zedong Thought Outer Red Guards, who weren't the objects of attack but of efforts to integrate them into the revolution. My sense of self-respect was hurt; I felt my enthusiasm for Mao and the Party was equal to anyone else's. But because of our different status, we weren't allowed to take part in certain activities, such as struggle sessions,[9] searching homes and confiscating things, and other important political actions. There was no way I could go along, and this really upset me. Originally I was class monitor, then overnight I was out. I was bursting to prove my devotion to the cause.

In 1969, when the call came to go to the countryside, I was the first to sign up and the first to put up a big-character poster,[10] asking to go to Inner Mongolia where living conditions were the hardest. At that time there were two options: In Heilongjiang you'd be sent to a state farm[11] and have the wages and benefits of a worker; in Inner Mongolia you'd be part of a production team[12] and treated as a peasant. I wanted to show that although I was an Outer Red Guard, I had just as much political consciousness as the rest of them. My family was behind me too. At that time, there wasn't a bit of coercion involved. The Chairman said youth should unite with workers, peasants, and soldiers! The thinking back then was that clear-cut and resolute. Now, though, it would probably be called ludicrously simple.

That move of mine set things in motion and got lots of people to sign up. But the school did something odd, and assigned me, who had signed up so eagerly, to Heilongjiang instead. Maybe it was a kind of reward, or maybe it was a tactic to get others to rush to sign up voluntarily instead of being ordered to go. Our three junior high classes and three high school classes, some 120 students in all, were organized into one company and sent to a state farm. I won't mention its name. They made me deputy company commander because, aside from the fact that I'd been the first to sign up, I'd been a class monitor and had some organizational ability. For instance, I wrote well and could speak in public. We were going to set out on August 16, but on the night of the fifteenth I suddenly developed a fever. Even the doctor never imagined that I would have an allergic reaction to the penicillin skin test he gave me. The safety coefficient of the test should be very high—probably not even one out of several ten thousands are at risk, and it had to be me. I immediately went into shock; my blood pressure dropped to twenty. That was a close call. They struggled frantically to save me, and I made it. When people from my school and others who had come from the state farm asked me if I could go, I said of course I could, even if I had to be carried on a stretcher. That's what my attitude was like then. The next afternoon, August 16, when I was helped onto the train by my family, my head was burning. I'd had a shot and packed some medicine and that's how I went.

7

Going to the Countryside then was completely different from what it was like later. It was voluntary then, and only later were people forced to go. Very few cried. I remember the scene perfectly: The station was filled with people seeing everybody off with drums and gongs. Of course some people did shed tears. But there was no sense of banishment, just the natural feelings when family members parted. The students on the train all helped each other out—everybody was chummy. By then there was no more distinction among Maoist Red Guards, Mao Zedong Thought Red Guards, and Mao Zedong Thought Outer Red Guards. We sang or recited quotes from Mao and shouted slogans all the way. The train was really alive with singing and dancing. For the great majority of us, it was the first time we'd ridden on a train in our lives. It was refreshing to watch the beauty of the landscape of our motherland along the way. It made us feel even more strongly that this was the only road for educated youth to take. That's the way we thought.

When we got to the Great Northern Wilderness, the first problem we faced was that working conditions were too harsh. The first real, direct challenge was survival itself. We very seldom ate flour or rice. Mostly we got so-called cornmeal and stuff, and every now and then they'd give us a little white flour, but very, very seldom. And the food was rationed. Every month we got thirty jin of meal,[13] but the work was so strenuous it wasn't nearly enough. Sometimes we were so hungry we couldn't stand it. We'd run over to the stables and steal the bean cakes they used for fodder. Strong guys like us could eat two jin in one meal when we were working. Working with empty stomachs, we got tired easily. The more tired we got, the hungrier we'd be, and the hungrier we were, the harder it was to get full—it was a vicious cycle. We had to get up every morning at three or four, and we worked till dark.

The farm had paddy fields, and its levels of mechanization was extremely low. All the tilling, sowing, and reaping had to be done manually. People were the machines. In the northwest, you prepare for planting in May, and first you have to till the land. For that you had to wear shorts, and on top you wore a cotton-padded jacket. Although the ice on top was completely melted and the water was only just over ten centimeters deep, the ground beneath was all mud and ice, and your feet got all cut up. I don't know if it was the ice or the cold water, but with the wind on top of that, your legs froze and the skin was covered with little cuts. One year I went home after spring planting. When my mother saw that the whole lower half of my body was covered with cuts, she felt so bad she cried. We didn't let the girls go into the water. When we boys did the planting we weren't allowed to wear boots for fear we'd trample the ground, so we had to go barefoot. At that time nobody was crazy about the idea, so we platoon leaders and company commanders had to take the lead. We'd work for a while and when we couldn't stand it any longer, we'd climb out, take a few swigs of "white lightning," and go back in.

Now, I don't even know what the hell we were thinking of back then. The day before yesterday I found a letter I wrote at the time. As soon as you read it you'll understand what it was all about in those days. This was a letter to my father, and of course it was a personal family letter.[14]

September 15, 1969

LONG LIVE CHAIRMAN MAO
Hi Dad!

I got your letter and have read it carefully. I'd like to share a few of my own thoughts with you below, and hope you'll criticize and correct my errors.

At the Tenth Plenary Session of the Eighth Central Committee of the Communist Party, our great leader Chairman Mao brilliantly pointed out that on the basis of Marxist-Leninist theory on class and class struggle, the "four existences"[15] would remain during the entire transition period in a socialist society. He stressed that we must discuss the "two-line struggle"[16] every year, every month, every day.

What you mentioned in your letter was a reflection of "two-line struggle." It's the uninterrupted pursuit of this kind of struggle that keeps our Party vigorous, for it strengthens the Party and promotes the progress of history. Chairman Mao said, "A momentary setback does not represent universal laws of history." Dad, you must not only struggle resolutely against certain bourgeois ill winds, but also be mentally prepared for long-term struggle, and stand a little higher, look a little farther.

Chairman Mao teaches us that we should believe in the masses and the Party, and I think you should completely rely on the Party, and accept the Party's guidance and teachings and truthfully report any problems you encounter in daily life to the next level of Party organization, without watering them down at all. Dad, we should be willing to sacrifice everything to defend Chairman Mao's revolutionary line. Chairman Mao's revolutionary line will surely prevail!

Also, a new revolutionary committee has been established in my province. The Central Committee was directly in charge of Heilongjiang and ferreted out X, exposed and criticized his terrible crimes, and launched an antirevisionism and rectification movement. Revolution is in full swing. X was guilty of four major crimes. He was:

1. A shameless traitor
2. A loyal running dog[17] of the KMT[18]
3. A counterrevolutionary revisionist

4. A chief culprit in opposing the Party and trying to take over the military

They've now begun a political examination of my application to join the Party. The branch secretary and other officials have come to talk with me and help me several times. I'm now in the process of intensifying my study to have a better understanding of the Party and truly join the Party in my heart. There are many intellectuals in the company, and hence many problems. I want to constantly strengthen my ideological reform and endeavor to season myself so that I will become a person who will give Chairman Mao no worries.

Take care of your health, Dad!

Long live the success of Chairman Mao's revolutionary line!

Your son,
XX

P.S. I received the things you asked my classmate to bring.

P.P.S. It's harvest time already and we're busy again. And it's beginning to get cold here.

Don't you think that letter's weird? That's how we students wrote back then. Every last one of us. And those things weren't written for outsiders, but for our own families. Revolution became part of everything.

Then something I'd never expected happened. Damn it—my little sister was raped.

It was the worst blow of my life. To this day my mother doesn't even know about it. My sister's husband—when you write about this be as vague as you can. Whatever you do, don't let them figure it out. If my mother learned about it now it would kill her. This is the biggest secret weighing on my heart.

It was the winter of 1970. Company members started taking turns to go back and visit their families. I didn't go—I had to take care of a whole pile of stuff involving the whole company. I was a cadre, so I had to be extra strict with myself when it came to my own needs and let others go first. It was at that time that I suddenly got a letter from my father. My little sister went to the countryside in 1969. She was too young, and she was sent to Hebei Province so she'd be closer to home and easier to look after. . . . Don't mention which county or farm. My father's letter was really a bolt from the blue. He said my sister had been raped by one of the production brigade's bookkeepers. At that time my sister was very active politically; she'd been named a county-level activist for the study of Mao's works and we often exchanged letters and encouragement. The news literally tore me up. My thoughts turned at once to how my sister was, how desperate, how sad! I didn't want anyone else to know, and I didn't dare cry out loud, I just muffled my sobs in my blankets at night. I was really afraid she would commit suicide. To tell the truth, she was just a girl, not yet sixteen. Though at the time I only had a vague idea of the facts of life, I could imagine that it must have destroyed her. I decided to ask for leave to go home, to see my parents, but mainly to rush to see my sister. I knew how much she needed me!

At that time, I decided to have my sister transfer to where I was. Just before I left I talked the matter with the head of the farm's revolutionary committee and gave him the letter to read. That leader was a pretty good guy. He expressed his sympathy on the spot, and said that as long as they would let her go, we could take care of it. But if they said no, it would be difficult. It seemed I had someone I could count on.

When I got home, my father and I went to see my sister. Of course we kept my mother in the dark about it. My mother's health wasn't good, and if she'd found out, it would definitely have made her worse.

My father told me the details of my sister's situation. What had happened? She lived in a small room all by herself, very close to the bookkeeper's house. That bookkeeper was in his thirties, and had a wife and kids. The first time he forced his way in at night, my sister fought him, but how could she fight against such a big, strong man? Afterward she didn't dare tell anyone. I understand. She was so young, all alone, without a single relative there with her. How was she to know what to do? She thought about dying, but didn't want to if her family would be in the dark about why. She was torn. But a few days later he came again, that bookkeeper. After the second time, my sister truly couldn't take it anymore, and she went and told a commune leader. The commune notified my father, who didn't know what to do either, so he wrote and told me.

When I saw my sister—to tell the truth, even now it makes me very sad to talk about it, and it was even sadder then. So I tried my best to convince my sister, whatever you do, don't kill yourself, it's not your fault.

My sister was staying with the chairwoman of the Women's Federation then. She was just lying there when we came in, and as soon as she saw me she buried her head and started crying. She was too young, just turned fifteen. I wanted to go and have it out with the man, one on one. So what if we both died? My father held me back. I ran over to the commune leaders and demanded that they punish him severely, and they agreed.

I took my sister home, and of course I told her, "Whatever you do, don't let Mom find out." I said, "I'll definitely get you out of there. As soon as I get back, I'll fix it up for you. Our leaders have all agreed. While you're at home, don't you dare think of doing anything foolish, because if anything happens you've got me to answer to."

A few days later I went back to my sister's commune to ask about the procedure for her transfer, and to demand again that they deal with that bookkeeper. Actually, they never touched him, even afterward. In the countryside, the bookkeepers control the finances, and they're tight with the production brigade cadres, local tyrants, every one of them! As far as I know, they haven't dealt with him to this day. You think I should go back again now? It'd be even more useless than it was then! It's been over ten years; too much time has passed.

That trip home I stayed over ten days in all, but not one of them was spent sitting idle. On a broken-down bicycle, I visited the homes of over a hundred boys and girls in our company. Sometimes I would find the house, but everyone would be at work, so I'd have to go back later. I was a company leader, wasn't I? I just wanted to let the parents know what was going on with their children, keep them from worrying. We were all so young and so far away from home, so what parents wouldn't worry? My mother was very concerned about me and complained that she never saw me. But it was my responsibility to do those things, especially when I looked at my sister and was reminded of other people's families.

My sister couldn't eat, and every night she screamed and cried in her sleep. She lost a lot of weight and became extremely skinny, and her face lost all its color. My mother could tell something was wrong, but she never imagined what was really going on. Later I transferred my sister to where I was. I was sure that once she was with me she'd be fine. But somehow rumors started spreading. It went all around that my sister was a girl of questionable morals who had only moved there because

THEY WHO HAVE SUFFERED GREATLY

she couldn't stay any longer where she had been. I can't say whether the rumors were started by the person who handled her transfer. It would have been all right if people had known what really happened, but the rumors had reached the point where I couldn't very well have explained the truth—that would have ended up just digging her in deeper. The girls in particular looked askance at my sister, and she gradually sensed it. She couldn't explain; all she could do was work harder and make strict demands on herself in every area. She rose to the top in both work and study—she cut a mu[19] and a half of wheat for every mu others cut and still couldn't make advanced worker. She tried time after time to get into the Youth League[20] but never made it; the girl comrades wouldn't vote for her because they always had the nagging suspicion that she was a bad girl who wouldn't have moved there unless she'd done something wrong. Somebody even asked the Party organization to investigate her history. The Party knew perfectly well what her situation was but didn't dare tell anyone. They were afraid it would be too shameful for my sister. Life is full of contradictions. People toss off cutting remarks over the littlest things, saying things like "you dirty so-and-so," "tramp," "slut," stuff like that. Sometimes my sister would come find me at night. We'd go walking in the bumpy, overgrown fields and she'd always cry. I never imagined that the move would be so hard for her. I felt like crying too, but I held back my tears. Away from our parents, I had a responsibility to her, and wouldn't my crying just hurt her? So I tried to give her some encouragement. I told her how our father was orphaned in his teens and how hard it had been for him to bring up his younger brother and sister, how our aunt had nearly been tricked into the whorehouse. "Anything can happen in life," I said, "but we have to go on living! What's more, we're better off than so many others, far better off than those living among the peasants in the production teams. And gradually, as the people here get to know you, their impression of you will change." I kept working on her like that, and it seemed to help—she gradually grew stronger.

Since I'm a very conscientious person and I stand up for my principles, I often offend people. Like everyone else, I'm not perfect either. So some people were always saying nasty things. Because of our particular circumstances, my sister and I were especially sensitive. I never gave my sister special consideration when it came to work—I've always felt that a little hardship never hurt anyone, and I couldn't do that, if only because I was a cadre. I had my sister work more than the others. She understood, and did everything I asked. I'm very grateful to her, really.

Some of the high school girls gradually came to appreciate what kind of people my sister and I were and stopped believing the rumors floating around. They told me that my sister often woke them all up in the middle of the night with her screams. They didn't know what had really happened, but they sensed that something was wrong, so they made allowances for her without being asked.

My sister's problems went on for two or three years. Fortunately, we made it through. Our work was outstanding, and we both made it into the Party. Later we were chosen to do office work.

I believe that what happened to my sister didn't happen to just a handful of the girls who went to the countryside at that time; it happened to thousands and thousands. Later, as those days were drawing to a close, when I worked in a Department of Organization[21] at the farm and was responsible for discipline and policy implementation, I came across many such cases. I discovered that many state farm cadres—they had the power—bullied the girls, and I read lots of briefs and documents on how these cases were handled. The head of the sixteenth regiment was executed because he alone had raped dozens of educated girls who'd been sent down. It wasn't just two or three at each state farm, and Heilongjiang had over a hundred farms. Nationwide, 20 million educated youths were sent to the countryside in those days, half of them girls—10 million. And a good many of them wouldn't talk about it even if it had happened to them. I'm not jumping to conclusions. In 1977, when cases were being reinvestigated, a veteran cadre at the farm asked for his to be. What was the issue? He'd been expelled from the Party for raping an educated girl who'd been sent to the countryside. The girl in question had gone off to college by then. The Department of Organization sent someone to find her and look into the matter, never imagining that she would refuse to admit it had ever happened. In fact, according to many details in the interrogation transcripts and case records, it really had. She just didn't want to have anything to do with it once she'd gotten a fresh start in life at college. That cadre probably figured she'd feel that way, and that's why he tried to get his conviction overturned. There was no proof, so there wasn't much we could do . . . and that's why I say there were thousands and thousands.

Of course there's nothing unusual about that sort of thing happening anywhere, anytime. But if we hadn't made such policy errors—if it hadn't been for political and economic factors that came about as a result of the Cultural Revolution—and sent so many educated youths off to the country, thus giving those horny bastards opportunities, I think the tragic misfortunes of many, many girls could have been avoided. I met so many girls like that back then—I really don't want to talk about it.

Our generation has paid too great a price. But I still think that "Going to the Countryside" had its positive aspect too. It's just that the price was too high, wouldn't you say?

Why do I still have such a positive outlook on life today? Because my life back then, despite its harshness, still had rewards, real, true rewards.

A lot of the Great Northern Wilderness was cultivated by us. Yes, and I'm proud of it. It was a new farm with nothing on it, just virgin land as far as the eye could see. Eighty percent of the farm was young people, and the rest consisted of a few army veterans from the fifties and their families. We were the mainstay. Naturally, the older generation had laid a foundation for us. Really, no matter how exhausted we were in spring, we were still elated when autumn came and the wheat was ripe and the grain went to market and the watermelons were in season and the pigs were fattened up, because we had done it all! That's why I say our youth wasn't totally lost. It had its value. Right?

Many of my comrades-in-arms never came back; they lost their lives. There were many reasons—some died fighting fires, some were murdered. These things happened to people I worked side by side with. An educated youth from Shanghai and I got an order at the same time, saying there was a subversive trying to sabotage the state farm and we had to catch him. It was a dark night. We were the ones to find him, and we chased him to the river. The young man from Shanghai had him cornered, and when the suspect saw he had no way out, he jumped into the water. It was April, and the river had just melted, though pieces of ice were still floating on the surface. This guy from Shanghai jumped in too, but he hadn't had a chance to take off his cotton-padded jacket. He swam and swam and then sank, and I watched him go under. The subversive drowned too. I'll never forget that battle. Can you say that this educated youth died a meaningless death? He was defending our country!

There's a huge forest in the Great Northern Wilderness, bigger than most of the ones in the central plains: It's got a circumference of several hundred li.[22] Every year in spring and autumn, fires break out easily there. What with the dried branches and rotten leaves, fires just start. Most of them were caused by carelessness—with campfires, cigarettes, or sparks from truck exhaust—and some started naturally. At the first sign of a fire, we would run out to fight it. People were badly burned and some were burned to death. Once a dormitory caught fire, and an educated youth died trying to put the fire out. The night before we'd bunked together, talking and laughing. A girder came crashing down and killed him instantly.

Some died of rabies after being bitten by mad dogs, and of various other illnesses. Their ashes are there to stay and, of course, so is the impact of their lives.

Thinking of them makes me realize that there are things about our generation that are really worth eulogizing. They're not fiction; they're all facts, facts close to home. Things I saw with my own eyes. Some writers come up with stuff like "Testimony of the Wilderness" or "Testimony of the White Birch Forest," but they needn't bother, there's no need; I'm a witness.

Another thing I'll mention is my joining the Party then. I had to file three applications before one was finally approved. Many ordinary soldiers had already succeeded in joining the Party. The reason for the delay in my case was the problem with my grandfather that I mentioned earlier. In the beginning, my father was so grateful to the Party for saving his life that he worked harder at his job to repay them, but when he tried to join the Party, his application was turned down for this same reason.

When I went to the farm Party committee to ask what the

problem with my grandfather was, they answered, "You say your grandfather was killed by an arms smuggler. What if that arms smuggler was part of a Red Army guerrilla detachment under the Communist Party? We have to be responsible to the Party!" To tell the truth, I never even laid eyes on my grandfather. He died when my father was fifteen.

Whether or not they let me into the Party, I worked hard just the same.

Some educated youths were always wavering in their commitment; they were always thinking about returning to the city. In fact, in the first year of "going to the countryside," children of high-ranking cadres relied on the influence of their parents to get them into the People's Liberation Army;[23] this was the first group. The second group had all kinds of ways out—a certain number were chosen to transfer to jobs or universities in the cities, some claimed special handicaps, some even managed to get transferred from farm work to factories in remote areas —sooner or later many, many of them left. I was determined to put down roots on the farm; I bit my finger and wrote an oath in blood to stay. I've got a document here from back then, take a look—"Work Team Brief." Back then certain outstanding youths were called "XX-style outstanding team members." XX was my name. In the end, the secretary of the Party Committee made the final decision; he said he'd take responsibility for any further problems with the business about my grandfather. So I joined the Party. I'll never forget that secretary. After I left there, he transferred to a government bureau and became bureau chief. He really knew what he was doing. He had three ribs broken in struggle sessions during the Cultural Revolution.

It was really hard for educated youths to transfer to the cities, especially the ones who had no way out. Watching everybody else leave one after another, they had to think of their own ways. What did the girls come up with? They resorted to marriage. They got engaged to somebody from a big city and then arranged their city residence cards;[24] love didn't enter into it at all. The boys were more desperate; there's no way to describe how they felt. With no way out, they manufactured illnesses, swallowed nails, or ate coins, which then showed up as shadows in the fluoroscopy. Or they cut their hands and dripped blood into their stools, or put a little egg white in their urine, so the tests came out positive. To tell the truth, it reached the point where they'd stop at nothing.

I remember a girl who was engaged to a worker in Beidagang. It was all arranged for her to go back and meet him over the May Day holiday. Most of the 100 or so members of the company went home for Spring Festival. I stayed. There were over a thousand pigs, several hundred sheep, and dozens of horses and cows, as well as many facilities that needed looking after. That girl stayed too, to save up a few more days of leave to use over May Day. She loved things to be clean. She was washing blankets in the dormitory. The room was quite warm and she was wearing thin clothes. Going outside a few times to fetch water, she caught a cold. Even several days of antibiotics did nothing to bring her fever down. We were worried, and took her to the hospital. Back then, the farm headquarters was miles away, and the electricity was out when they needed to do lab tests. So we carried her to the county hospital. A week had passed before she got proper treatment. By then she could no longer produce blood; she had aplastic anemia. I took along two boys and two girls and the five of us looked after her. She needed constant blood transfusions. I decided that the girls shouldn't give blood, and when we three boys had our blood tested, we found that one boy and I had type O. But he looked a little reluctant about it, so I said I'd give blood. I gave 400 cc, and the color came back into her face where it had been a yellowish green before. She perked up in no time. I spent the whole day squatting in the hallway. The doctor said to her, "That boyfriend of yours is really something." She replied, "He's our political instructor, not my boyfriend." The doctor was really moved, and insisted on giving me a bed so I could get some sleep. We didn't close our eyes for nine days and nine nights.

Despite all our efforts, we couldn't save her. After she died she was cremated in Harbin. When I returned after taking care of the funeral, people told me, "You look like hell." I looked as if I'd just come out of jail. On her deathbed, that girl held onto my hand and wouldn't let me leave. By then, her older sister and her brother-in-law had been contacted by telegram and rushed to see her, but they weren't allowed into the room during treatment. She had had a bit of a falling-out with them. She wouldn't let go of me. Her eyes stayed fixed on me and there were tears streaming down her face. By that point she could no longer speak, but she was still conscious. I was crying too. Our relationship wasn't one of lovers at all; we were like brother and sister. At that time my only thought was how to keep her alive. I felt we had suffered enough. She had fallen ill and couldn't even get to see her parents. With my own eyes, I watched her stop breathing. In Harbin, I carried the urn that held her ashes—it was still warm—and I thought, I would give any amount of blood if only she could live.

Thousands and thousands of girl comrades took that route. For those who had sacrificed love and dignity and the rights people ought to have for a way out, things weren't necessarily good. Because there was no love in that way out and that kind of seed was bound to produce bad fruit. And that was another tragedy for the girls. Their worth lay only in the fact that they were female. All we rough-and-tumble boys could do was destroy ourselves, swallow nails, and so on. I always yelled at people who did that: "We can't do that! If you can't stand the hardship, you don't deserve to live."

Almost all the educated youths had returned to the cities in 1979. I was the last of the company to go. When I left I felt guilty. I felt that even though I was the last to leave I was still a deserter, that in the end I had fought a losing battle, or that I hadn't been able to conquer myself, that I still had to follow the crowd. My family wanted me to come back. The place was nearly empty, and the dormitory was lonely as hell. At the time, the greatest pressure was loneliness. When a big group of hoods from Shandong, Hebei, and Henan came to take jobs as temporary workers, I was in charge of them, but it didn't feel right. I thought, I've got to go.

I'll never forget my last day there. Dozens of veteran farm workers saw me off. I was carrying one bag—all it had in it were some worn-out clothes and a few old books and such. As we left the barracks and crossed that little bridge, it was like a funeral procession—they followed behind me, crying. Some buried their faces in their hands and sobbed. Even though they were ignorant and uncultured, if you compared the way they related to each other with the way city people did, these people were wonderful! They saw me off a long, long way, and I could still hear them crying after I had left them behind.

When I got back, for a long time I couldn't eat and didn't sleep well—everything was like a dream. In theory, you should eat and sleep better at home, but I just felt empty, as if I had lost many, many things. Later I felt I shouldn't be that way, that I should start over from the beginning. People have to start from wherever they are. And that's how I gradually regained my positive attitude toward life. Didn't I tell you I like literature? Besides working hard at my job, in 1980 I took lit classes at the Cultural Palace[25] in my spare time. In 1982, I started studying at a TV college.[26] I graduated last year. I don't want to boast, but I have to admit my academic record was satisfactory. I worked so hard because I was afraid of losing my identity. I'm studying literature for a reason. I think I have a responsibility to express myself and my generation. I'll never be a millionaire, and I'll never leave my son any property to speak of. But if while I'm alive I can leave behind a book, then I won't have lived my life in vain.

Those years left me in bad health. My arthritis often acts up, and my stomach too, and when they hurt I just . . . put up with it. Those aches and pains will probably be with me for the rest of my life.

My sister got married a long time ago, but has never been able to tell her husband about what happened back then. If she hasn't told him by now, it's better not to. There's much more buried in our hearts than that pain. But I think our generation is a great one. And I'm not just trying to console myself. Back then, the Cultural Revolution made such a mess of the national economy that it nearly collapsed, and if we hadn't gone to the countryside, 20 million people would have been an awful burden on the cities. Even if we were duped, even if we suffered, we still supported a part of the national structure that was on the verge of collapse; wouldn't you say? It should be said that our generation bore the brunt of the Cultural Revolution. We were the ones. But to this day, there has never been a correct appraisal of the Going to the Countryside Movement. I wrote a poem once; the manuscript's long gone. But I remember some lines; they went something like this:

When it should have been lush with leaves
They fell too soon;
It supports a corner of the falling sky
Though its trunk is covered with scars.

I know that poem's immature. But it expresses what I really think, my beliefs, my strength. And so I say that what our generation has lost and gained are equally important. Our lives weren't wasted. We'll never forget the Great Northern Wilderness. We left so many things there, and we brought so many things back. Wouldn't you say?

It has always been the people, not the sages, who rescued the country from disaster.—F. J.

FOOTNOTES

1. During the early part of the Cultural Revolution, all schools, universities, and work units were organized along military lines, i.e., team, platoon, company, battalion, regiment, and division.

2. Heilongjiang is a province of northeast China bordering the Soviet Union at the Amur River. The farm referred to was an undeveloped area of the Great Northern Wilderness—mostly wasteland and swamps.

3. On May 7, 1968, at the beginning of the Cultural Revolution, Chairman Mao issued a directive calling on all educated urban youths

to go to the countryside to settle, unite with the peasants, and be reeducated by them.

4. In 1949, the People's Liberation Army, led by Mao Zedong, defeated the Nationalist Army led by Chiang Kai-shek, and founded the People's Republic of China.

5. "Monster" was a common epithet used during the Cultural Revolution for those considered extreme enemies of the working class.

6. Red Guards were members of a mass organization, initiated at Chairman Mao's behest, which consisted of young people—mostly of high school and college age—and was dedicated to safeguarding the dictatorship of the proletariat and "Mao Zedong thought." They would take action against those they regarded as enemies of these things, and played a major role in turning the Cultural Revolution into a nationwide mass movement.

7. Cadres means leaders.

8. The five black categories consisted of landlords, rich peasants, counterrevolutionaries, Rightists, and "bad elements."

9. Struggle sessions were meetings held in public to denounce someone, and enumerate his or her crimes. These meetings usually involved physical punishment and humiliation.

10. A poster written in bold characters with ink and brush used during the Cultural Revolution for purposes of denouncing someone, airing complaints, and urging the masses to do likewise.

11. A farm owned and operated by the state.

12. An organization composed of farmers who worked together under the jurisdiction of the commune.

13. One jin equals half a kilogram, or a little more than one pound.

14. During the early phases of the Cultural Revolution, Chinese citizens, at the urging of Lin Biao, praised Chairman Mao and quoted him when writing letters, greeting one another, and the like.

15. Defined in a speech given by Chairman Mao in 1962 as consisting of (a) classes, class contradictions, and class struggles, (b) the struggle between the socialist and capitalist paths, (c) the danger of

the restoration of capitalism, and *(d)* the danger of invasion or sabotage by imperialists.

16. "Two-line struggle" refers to the conflict between differing political and ideological viewpoints within the Party.

17. Negative term for devoted and blind follower.

18. The Kuomintang (often abbreviated as KMT) was founded by Dr. Sun Yat-sen and later headed by Chiang Kai-shek. This was the party Mao ousted from power in 1949.

19. 1 mu equals 0.1647 acres.

20. The Communist Youth League is an organization affiliated with the Communist Party for young people who aspire to further the cause of communism but are not yet old enough to join the Party.

21. A Department of Organization oversees the performance, discipline, punishment, and rehabilitation of those under its supervision.

22. One li equals half a kilometer.

23. The army of the Communist Party, which, since defeating the Kuomintang in 1949, has been the only official army of the People's Republic of China; the name is often abbreviated as PLA.

24. A residence card is a document that both allows a Chinese citizen to live in a particular place and restricts him or her to living in that place.

25. An organization offering spare-time recreational and educational activities.

26. A college in which the courses are given by television to students working toward a college degree.

AVENGER

TIME: *1966* ❦ AGE: *25* ❦ SEX: *Male*
OCCUPATION: *Cadre in the production section of a factory in T city*

At the moment I'm taking a course on law in the State Lawyer's Center part-time in the evenings. Don't think I'm becoming a lawyer to change my job. Certainly not. To tell you the honest truth, the only reason I'm studying law is to get revenge. Why revenge? You just listen to my story.

I graduated from a technical school of mechanical engineering in 1963. I stepped out of the school door into a factory. I was assigned to work as a cadre in charge of production. At that time there were only three people in my section: the section chief, who was invariably away at meetings, a statistician, and me. Don't think I'm boasting. I'm not stupid; actually I'm quite capable and can still accomplish something now if I try. Soon after I joined the section, all the things the factory manager was not taking care of like molds, tools, production plans, and quality control came under my supervision. As a new graduate, I was very honest, knew nothing about greasing palms and always stuck to the rules. To use a modern expression, I lacked tact. I'll give you an example. Someone came to me for an approval to requisition some tools. I recognized him and told him that he'd just gotten some a few days ago. I refused to give him any more. Because of this, he held a grudge against me. There were quite a number of cases like that. I was too dumb to realize that I had sown the seeds of trouble.

As soon as the Cultural Revolution started, the people who had stored up their resentments against me began to look for faults. At first, they couldn't find any because of my impeccable record in the factory. However, every dog has its day. No one was really to blame but myself. One day I was copying one of Chairman Mao's quotations as the heading for a big-character poster and somehow botched it. The sentence goes: "Whatever the enemy opposes, we should uphold." But I wrote: "Whatever the enemy opposes, we should oppose." This was one of Mao's most often quoted sayings. How I got it wrong, I still can't figure out. Perhaps the sentence is a bit of a tongue twister or maybe it just wasn't my day. It was really playing with fire and begging for trouble. The characters were there in black and white. You couldn't deny them. To "oppose Mao Zedong thought" meant you were an active counterrevolutionary and being a counterrevolutionary was the worst of all political crimes. Rightists, spies, traitors, and capitalists were tigers that had been killed while an active counterrevolutionary was a real live one that people could do something about. I was literally sending myself to the guillotine, to use the phrase popular then. I seriously considered ending my own life.

I was exposed on the spot and then was subjected to denunciations at big and small meetings and daily beatings. My tormentors were the workers known for their cunning and malicious behavior. They were all huge brutes. Though I was twenty-five, I still couldn't take so much beating. I'd never had any physical training and had never developed any resistance to violence. They claimed that even if they beat me to death, nothing would happen to them since so many others had already been killed elsewhere and nothing had been done.

These workers had seldom done any work in the past. Now they'd found themselves something that suited them—beating others as they pleased. They'd beat us in the evenings—on the body so as not to show any evidence on our faces. We were given a little food but hardly any water. You know, a man can live without food for a while but will soon die without water. I wasn't even allowed to piss properly. I had to make a container with a piece of paper, piss in it, and then dump it in the corner of the "cowshed."[1] Meanwhile the bastards would be standing outside watching me suffer. I think they got a kick out of it.

They also came up with another ingenious method of torturing us. We'd be shut in the "cowshed" and forced to slap each other. If someone didn't slap hard enough, he'd be singled out for a good beating. This way they'd get us beaten without even lifting a finger. They really enjoyed the sight of our swollen black-and-blue faces.

One day, I don't know what possessed them, but they suddenly decided to cut off my penis with a pair of scissors. Of course I couldn't let them do that to me. I hadn't gotten married yet and now my life would really be finished. I resisted with all the strength I had left, holding onto my pants as tightly as I could. My hands were bleeding from the scissors and perhaps the sight of blood stopped them. In any event, I kept my penis. My ears suffered too. They were deformed by their pliers. You take a look at them. They look like cauliflowers now.

The so-called military propaganda team also joined in. They came to the factory supposedly to propagate "Mao Zedong thought" but used their authority to beat people at will. They liked to try out their hand-to-hand combat techniques on us. I was driven crazy by their mauling. Finally I slipped into the clinic and stole dozens of tranquilizers. I took them all at once, but they didn't do the trick. I don't know if I was fortunate or hadn't suffered enough yet. "Committing suicide to escape punishment" was my latest crime and I received even more beatings for my trouble. The worst torture was not being allowed to sleep at night. Instead we were forced to stand and bend over with our arms rigidly lifted upward behind us. It was called the "airplane." A single movement anywhere would bring down a blow on that part of the body. I swallowed pesticide. I tried escape. Nothing worked. Each attempt only led to worse punishment. My health broke down from those beatings and has never recovered. I'm telling you this because, at least until now, I haven't been able to find any other form of release. Those people were just too evil.

Of the people who persecuted me, some had grudges against me. I told you that. But some I'd never had anything to do with directly. So why did they treat me so cruelly? I believe everybody had his or her own axe to grind. Let me tell you a story. My father and my mother's sister's family lived together. My father and aunt were on bad terms. One day while chatting, my father remarked that we should watch what we said in public. It might cause trouble. Later my aunt wrote an anonymous letter to his work unit. In it she claimed that my father had said there was no freedom of speech in our socialist society. As a result, my father was sent off to the countryside to do manual labor. When the Cultural Revolution came, he was further disgraced by being sent back to his hometown in Hunan Province. I had visited him once. He was doing forced hard labor in the village with a label of "counterrevolutionary" sewn to the front of his clothes. He also attempted suicide several times. He was in a wretched state. I'm sure you'd have been heartbroken if you'd seen him then. In those days tragedy could hit you unexpectedly anytime. I deeply appreciate the old saying: "Misfortune strikes out of the blue."

Some of my persecutors were temporary workers. By taking part in the process of "revolution," they hoped to become full-time employees. Some others had jobs in workshops. What they had in mind was getting transferred to office work. All of them had personal motives. The Cultural Revolution provided them with an opportunity to achieve their ends. Some succeeded and got promoted on the backs of others. I was one of their stepping-stones. Hell, it was my fate.

Oh yes, there was another reason for their cruelty to me. The director of the revolutionary committee of the factory wanted to put a group of people supporting him in power. I was in charge of production, so I had some real power. They meant to kick me out and put one of their own in my place. The charge that I was a counterrevolutionary distorting Chairman Mao's words was merely a pretext. Only by getting rid of one group of people could you replace them with another. It happened in many places. Once the revolutionaries of the moment eliminated the people then in power, they'd form a clique to oppose the other factions.

After 1973 my situation improved a bit. They'd gotten what they wanted, the power to control the whole factory, so there was no longer any need for them to regard me as a threat. They stopped calling me a counterrevolutionary and I was allowed to work in the workshop. In 1975 I was sent to nearby Baodi County to help develop a local factory.

I met an old worker there who thought I was an honest person. The people sent there with me also vouched for me. The old worker decided to marry off his daughter to me. The girl was an agricultural technician. An honest type. We got married. Returning to the city, we had no place to live. We squatted in the reception office of the factory warehouse. During the day the room was occupied by the warehouse watchman, and at night it was ours. A tiny little place to call home.

Some gossip started spreading about my father's and my counterrevolutionary background and eventually it reached my wife. They also said that she'd been made a scapegoat and would suffer for the rest of her life because of me. Coming from the countryside, she didn't know much about what had happened in the cities. However, the meaning of the word "counterrevolutionary" had been impressed on her. From that moment on, she started crying and fighting with me every day, accusing me of misleading her. What could I do? No matter what I told her she continued to doubt me, and finally believed that I really was a counterrevolutionary out to ruin her. We quarreled on and on and I could see she was suffering enormous mental pressure. She looked like I must have looked when I was undergoing my torments. We tried our best to stop fighting, but the word "counterrevolutionary" continued to haunt her.

She died suddenly from a heart attack eight months after our baby was born. She'd been quite healthy until then and never had any heart disease before. I understood that she died from neurotic depression. It really shouldn't have happened. It was because of me. Even though she was still employed by the factory at the time of her death, the factory refused to give me my death benefits because I was still considered problematic. I had to take care of the baby myself—be both father and mother. But what could a man do with such a young child? I kept the baby in the factory nursery most of the time. When my son reached school age, I married again. A child needs to be looked after properly. Yes, you're right. A stepmother is never as good as the real one. No matter how nice my present wife is, she and the boy will never be very close. This has been a thorn in my side, but I'll just have to live with it. Who did I offend to deserve this? Who?

I was so horribly persecuted during the Cultural Revolution. But up to now, I still haven't been given a public rehabilitation because the power is still in the hands of those persecutors and exoneration for me means a disgrace to them. Besides, they're afraid I would resume my position and they'd have to give their power to me. Obviously they can't put me back in an important position because I might rock the boat too much.

Why do the people who led the persecutions always manage to keep their power? Why, because on the one hand, they have their power base in those dependent on them, and on the other, they are kept secure by the backing of those at the top whom they support. Even today, so long as they don't break the law, there's nothing you can do about them, is there? No way. If you're determined to go against them, one way or another they'll find ways to deal with you. Oh, you won't get beaten these days. They're not that stupid. But who can tell what they'd do if the Cultural Revolution ever occurred again.

My luck is so damn bad. But all those people who made me suffer, hey, they're all living like fat cats. Some of them are leaders and some are even in charge of the factory. Some got promotions and raises. They're useless when it comes to production, but real good at dirty deals with the country production teams. Their pockets are all jingling.

I'll tell you about them one by one. One guy's become the section chief of sales and purchasing, another's head of personnel, and still another is in charge of production. He gave me the worst beatings. The personnel head is the one who refused to give me water in the "cowshed." He used to be responsible for finance, but since he couldn't even put two and two together, accounting was a real headache. So he got himself transferred to personnel.

The Cultural Revolution really came down to the incompetent crushing the capable. They wouldn't have had a chance of getting promoted if they hadn't found a way to squeeze out their betters. The Cultural Revolution gave them that rare chance. The Gang of Four[2] was too lofty to have much effect on us ordinary people. Our real tormentors were the gangs in our own work units. You can see for yourself the mess they've made of things. The factory is really quite big and has a lot of potential, but it's flat broke. There's not so much as an extra pen refill to spare. Reform won't get anywhere in the hands of that bunch. I'll be damned if it does. But who am I to say anything? They've got supporters everywhere. So, the hell with them.

I finally decided to get myself transferred to a new work unit. They were overjoyed to see me go. Even though I never made trouble, I was still a pain in the ass to them. The investigation of the Gang of Four's supporters wasn't worth a good fart. Only those who didn't have enough connections were ferreted out. The rest got off scot-free. They've put on a new face and are getting along quite well. Now the catch phrase "looking forward into the future" is on everyone's tongue. This suits them just fine. They're only too happy to bury that horrible past. If you even mention the Cultural Revolution to them, they'll self-righteously accuse you of sabotaging the country's unity and stability.

Well, who in hell sabotaged who? My family's ruined. My wife's dead. My son's motherless. Twenty years have gone by since the Cultural Revolution and I'm over forty now. Somehow I've kept my body together, but my mind will never be the same again. Those bastards are still enjoying themselves to their heart's content. They've got everything—family, position, power, and the money that goes with it. What in hell can I do about it?

Oh, yeah. I do want to tell you something about two of the bastards. One was once a standing member of the factory revolutionary committee in charge of political work. The other was a workshop director. Both of them were prosecuted for rape. I reckon the law is the only way to get these guys. Nothing else works. They're all too slippery. They can always find loopholes in the country's policies and come out on top of any political movement. That's why I'm studying law. Rule by law is stressed very much today. I'm going to become an expert and wait patiently until one of them breaks the law. They're bound to do it and then I'll see that they get what they deserve. What's that you say? You think they're too clever to get caught in a criminal act? Damn it! Why can't you say something to help me? You think of a good idea, then, anything at all, as long as I can get my revenge!

"The weak rely upon the law, but who makes the law?"—F. J.

FOOTNOTES

1. A room reserved for the punishment of class enemies. The term derives from the use of the term "cow"—along with "snake," "monster," and "demon"—to refer to class enemies.

2. Four Party leaders—Mao's wife Jiang Qing, Zhang Qunqiao, Yao Wenyuan, and Wang Hongwen—who formed a faction within the Party and sought to seize the highest power during the Cultural Revolution. They were ousted in 1976 at the end of the Cultural Revolution.

WAS I REALLY GUILTY?

TIME: *1966* ✤ AGE: *30* ✤ SEX: *Female*
OCCUPATION: *Doctor in the Children's Hospital of T city*

I killed my father with my own hands. You already know this.

I was planning to talk with you a couple of days ago. I had to get it out. But last night I didn't have a wink of sleep, so I decided not to say anything today. Just the thought of recalling what happened and the way my parents looked on that day brings everything back too clearly. It's too painful. I'm hypertensive and was afraid that I wouldn't be able to handle this interview. But as soon as I met you, I knew I just had to talk. I've got to say something. Perhaps it's better this way.

My wounds can never be healed. Even after twenty years I

still can't figure out whether I was right to kill my father. My initial sentence was life imprisonment. However, when the Gang of Four fell, I was declared innocent and released. But was I really guilty or not? My family, my brothers and sisters-in-law, all told me they understood. But after all, I was the one who ended my father's life. If not for me, he certainly would have lived until now. He had been very healthy. Did I rescue him or destroy him? One moment I feel as though I did the right thing, but the next I'm bitterly remorseful. Why is it like that? At the time it all happened, I was not in my right mind. I had a complete nervous breakdown. Everything seemed unreal, chaotic, totally confused.

Back then, my two older brothers lived on the ground floor and my parents had the upstairs floor. I was working as a doctor in the Children's Hospital. I was also an active member of the Communist Youth League. I was diligent in my profession and had even received awards as a model worker. When all this happened I was staying with my parents on sick leave after contracting hepatitis while working in the countryside with my medical team.

It was on the morning of the twenty-sixth of August, 1966. Oh no, it was the twenty-eighth. The twenty-sixth was the beginning of the ransacking of my home. It was also the climax of the ransacking in the city. Our door was suddenly forced open by a group of middle-school Red Guards armed with clubs. They declared that my father was a capitalist. In fact, it was a misnomer. My father had inherited a house from his parents and rented out a vacant room on the ground floor. At most he could be called a householder. But in those days renting was synonymous with exploitation, that is, profiting without labor. Within minutes the Red Guards had smashed everything in my home to bits. My whole family was forced to kneel down in the hallway. We were all very naive and had no experience of such violent abuse. We were scared out of our wits. My father was a painter and had had one of his paintings displayed in America before 1949. The Red Guards examined the certificate from the American exhibition and said, "Aha! So you've got imperialist connections! You must be a dirty spy!" We were frightened to death. Only schoolchildren, you might think. Why were we so frightened? Well, during the Cultural Revolution almost all the families in our neighborhood were molested and had their houses ransacked. If those Red Guards felt like it, they could execute you on the spot. Everyone was terrified. One bunch after another would raid the houses. They'd smash everything. Books, paintings, anything that struck them as bourgeois would be taken out and burned. Then they would seal up your house. So many, many of them. Their bonfires were everywhere.

From the twenty-sixth to the twenty-eighth, from dawn to dusk, my parents and I were locked up and beaten with belts. Our hair was shorn to the roots. We were dragged out to the street again and again to be denounced and humiliated before the neighborhood. We never had a moment's peace. They tormented us ceaselessly until we no longer even felt a semblance of humanity. Suddenly we had somehow become enemies of our country. Just cringing there. No idea of what our monstrous crimes must be. Oh, how we longed to find a refuge, but where? The whole city was like this. Red Guards everywhere parading people in the streets to the sounds of gongs and drums. Tension was mounting rapidly and we had reached our breaking point. Even death seemed preferable to this.

Until the twenty-eighth, for three entire days, my parents and I had nothing to eat. Even our bowls had been smashed. It was only when the Red Guards left to eat that we were able to hurriedly make some noodle soup to feed my brother's children —straight out of the wok. That night my parents and I were filled with terror and despair. At daybreak the Red Guards would show up again. More denunciations, more humiliating parades, more physical torture. Too much to face. There was no way out. So the three of us made up our minds to die together.

It was pitch black. The power had been cut off—perhaps to prevent us from electrocuting ourselves. We were sitting on the foyer floor, racking our brains for a way to kill ourselves. It was raining outside. Already past midnight. Day would soon break; no time to waste. I felt a pocket knife on the floor attached to a key chain. The Red Guards must have missed it in their search. The knife seemed to be a godsend. I'm a doctor. I know that if you puncture the carotid artery in the neck, the embolism produced will result in immediate death. This was the fastest and most effective way. My father asked whether it would really work and I assured him it would. My mother said how lucky they were to have a doctor daughter to help them die. Since I was the doctor, we decided that I'd kill them first and then do it to myself. But things didn't turn out as we expected.

Before going through with it, we sat there hand in hand for God knows how long. The thought of parting forever was almost too much. I'd always been so close to my parents. They wanted me to help them die but to stay alive myself. That wouldn't do, I said. I'd be accused of murder and put to death anyway. The pass we had come to is unbearable to recall. As soon as I close my eyes, even the tiniest details come back to me. It was getting too late, already dawn. My parents both insisted that I go ahead with it. I had never thought myself capable of killing anyone, let alone my parents. But under these circumstances I was capable of it, and I had no other choice. My father encouraged me. He told me, "What you must do is something good. You will relieve our sufferings. Mother and I can't stand any more torturing when the Red Guards come again." My mind was too shattered. I felt compelled to do it.

I scrabbled about and found a crayon and two pieces of paper. In the lifting darkness I somehow managed to write out two suicide notes for the sake of my remaining family:

> We are the common enemy of the people. In order not to poison others surrounding us, we are determined to be liquidated from society. Long live the Great Proletarian Cultural Revolution!
>
> To XXX (my husband who was working in another city) and the Mu families (the families of my brothers who I didn't dare to identify as brothers for their own protection): You are resolutely following the revolutionary road. We are the sole cause of your trouble.

My father asked my mother to be first and she asked him the same, for whoever was first to die would be spared at least one grief. Finally father agreed to listen to mother one last time. He'd be the first to die.

I felt for my father's strong artery and pierced it. Immediately the hot blood spurted out. He even asked me to see if his pulse had stopped. I said that as far as I knew, it would be over in a minute. He said he wished it could be faster. Then my mother asked me if I was sure I could do it to myself. She knew I had to die with them; I couldn't be left behind. I reassured her that when they were finished, I'd die too. She waited there patiently as though I was about to give her medical treatment. We'd tried to be very quiet, not to alarm others. But suddenly one of my brothers ran upstairs yelling like a madman. It sounded as if the Red Guards were coming. He came and held me tight. All of a sudden I realized that I couldn't go on with this. I nearly fainted, but managed to struggle free. I ran to the third floor balcony and jumped. If I had hit headfirst, I'd have died. But there was no time even to think about how to jump or what would happen to my mother. I only remember hearing all the sounds of hell and then nothing.

It's like I told you. We were really being driven out of our minds. Mother and I hadn't planned to jump out the window. It just happened. When you reach the end, you close your eyes and do the obvious thing like we did. We jumped.

When I finally came to, I was still only half conscious. I thought I heard some voices. Maybe Red Guards. I don't know. When I opened my eyes for a second time, I was already in a hospital. I saw my mother and father lying beside me. But no, I was hallucinating. I shut my eyes, very scared, trying to think. This can't be. What happens if my father was saved? Faintly I could make out the babble of denunciation meetings and parades outside. In desperation I tried to concentrate. This was a women's ward. My father couldn't be here. My eyes were playing tricks on me. I didn't want to look again. My head was full of a cacophony of sounds. I think that it must have been a symptom of my mental disorder. I even tried to cry out, but somehow no sound came out of me. Afterward, the next time I came to, someone was questioning me about my case. I forget what he said.

When I fully regained consciousness, I was told that my mother had jumped off the balcony right after me. Later when I was being interrogated, I was told Father had died on the spot but Mother had been saved. How I cried for my dead father and also for my mother. I was badly injured and she was so old. She would be paralyzed or worse if she really had survived. It was only after the Cultural Revolution had ended and I was finally released that my sister-in-law told me the truth. My mother hadn't died right away. Instead they took her to the hospital, but she was refused treatment. You probably know that at that time people without a socially acceptable family background weren't admitted. Sometimes the hospitals even organized the "respectable" patients to denounce and criticize those "bad elements" who had earlier gained admission. I was admitted only because I had to face legal proceedings. My mother died a few days later at home. My father had died as they said and was cremated a week later.

The hospital didn't want to treat a patient like me. Very soon I was transferred to a prison hospital called New Life Hospital. Both of my legs were broken—the left tibia and the right femur. The right leg was more seriously injured, with a compression fracture. The bone had splintered and compressed so that the fragments overlapped, shortening the leg. The first hospital had applied skeletal traction, using a ten kilo sandbag to pull the bone back into position. But when I was moved to the prison, the hospital insisted I leave the bag behind. So the doctor put the bone fragments back into the wrong position. Just like breaking it again. It was only a sandbag. They could at least have let me use it, but no, they refused. That hospital didn't give a damn about me. Neither did the doctor who treated me. I don't know where he is now, but I hope he's no longer practicing medicine. What treatment I did get I was given only so that I could face my legal responsibility. It's strange to think about it now. My broken bones were pulled this way and that. But I felt no pain, not even a little. Didn't cry either. It was as if I was dead.

It was eleven o'clock when we arrived at the prison. The prison hospital staff didn't start working until two in the afternoon. When they finally came on, they separated my bone again and put in a steel pin. Then they manipulated the leg back and forth in the splint they made. My leg is still deformed. Only about a fifth of the bone has knitted. It aches a lot. I don't want to dwell on it. You can see I'm crippled for life.

I was formally arrested ten days later and handcuffed. That was September 7, 1966. In 1968 when the Military Control Commission[1] took over, I was charged with "committing the crime of murder in opposition to the Great Proletarian Cultural Revolution." Murder was a criminal offense and opposition to the Cultural Revolution was a political crime. A very serious combination. I was sentenced to life imprisonment. I thought then that I'd rather get the death penalty. Life imprisonment meant continuing to suffer. Here, you have a look at my sentence:

> It is verified that the accused Y, of a bourgeois family background, has failed to be reformed after Liberation. During the Great Proletarian Cultural Revolution, she has masterminded a scheme to resist the Great Proletarian Cultural Revolution through collective suicide and the murder of YY and furthermore has attempted personal suicide as a means of escaping punishment. The accused has both alienated herself from society and become an enemy of the people, thus committing the crime of murder in opposition to the Great Proletarian Cultural Revolution. In view of the seriousness of this offense, the vile manner in which it was committed, and the irrefutable evidence presented, this court, in solidarity with the proletarian dictatorship and the resolute defense of the Great Proletarian Cultural Revolution's continuing progress, hereby finds the accused guilty of murder in opposition to the Great Proletarian Cultural Revolution. The accused is sentenced to life imprisonment.

Someone from the commission said to me that if I had been just an ordinary housewife, my sentence wouldn't have been so severe. Obviously, however, I knew what I was doing. My father's case was considered very serious. He said I killed my father to save him from just punishment. That's the real reason I was sentenced to the crime of opposition to the Cultural Revolution.

Well, they said I killed my father to protect him. It's true. I did. This has been a great weight on my mind. What they meant is not the way I look at it. I saved my father from more torture, but they said I was guilty because I prevented them from torturing him anymore. Am I making myself clear? It's all very muddled. I've never been able to make any sense of it.

I was in prison for twelve and a half years. The only reason I didn't kill myself was that I always believed my mother was still alive. I tried to imagine how she was living. The three of us had planned to die together. My father, dead. Me, imprisoned for life. My mother—well, I'd never see her again. Every time my nephews came to visit me they'd tell me that Grandma was at home. Grandma wanted me to reform myself, they said, so that my sentence might be reduced. Sometimes even the prison guards would ask me to tell them about my mother. Of course, they knew my mother was dead, but they too tried to hide it from me. In fact I really had wished that my mother would have died. To live on was only more misery and suffering. If only I had been told the truth, I would have been at peace.

Once you've been in prison, you get a different perspective on things. I wouldn't have believed that so many good people could be so unjustly imprisoned until I saw them myself. My case, though, was different. I did kill my father with my own hands. I really wanted to atone for my sin, but I also hoped to get an early release so I could see my mother. I felt extremely guilty too toward my brothers. We have the same father but different mothers. However, we were so close that no one ever suspected. They never showed any hatred to me after Father died. They would often come to see me and send me food. Ah, each time I saw them I cried until I ran out of tears. I didn't know what to say. I felt I had betrayed them. But my brothers reassured me that they understood and that as long as they and my sisters-in-law lived, they'd never stop caring about me. For my brothers' sake also I really had to redeem myself. I worked as hard as I could to reform.

At first I was given sewing to do. I didn't even know how to use a sewing machine, so I started from square one. Pretty soon I got skilled at it. To sew collars was the hardest. Since I had become the best worker, I was given the difficult and important tasks. I even managed to exceed the quotas. We also did things like produce slogan posters, propaganda articles, and political drawings. I tried to lend a hand at everything. For production I was sometimes awarded a Red Flag or Chairman Mao's "Little Red Book."[2] Hey, have a look at my glasses. Can you guess how strong they are? I got nearsighted from looking at my sewing in those days.

I was also called upon to use my medical skills. It wasn't only to treat fellow prisoners, but also the chief warden and his children. If the ordinary prison workers, along with their relatives and cadre friends, called upon me, I'd go at a moment's notice too. To feel trusted by others, not regarded as an enemy —that was a great consolation. In the middle of the night I'd often be awakened to treat someone's fever, stomachache, or convulsions. It always took at least a few hours, but the next day I'd be off to work as usual. I was working like mad both day and night. The prison workers showed their appreciation. Even today they still sometimes come to see me at the hospital to have me treat their children. Back then, not being treated too harshly was the best I could ask for. Please don't laugh at me. At the slightest praise I'd be overjoyed for days.

There's one thing I want to mention. When I was officially arrested on the seventh of September, 1966, in the prison hospital, I was still married. My husband was working in Beijing. The weather was getting cold, I thought, and his clothes and belongings had already been taken away when our apartment was ransacked. He shouldn't suffer anymore because of me. So I wrote a letter asking him to arrange a divorce. By the end of September, it came through. Not long after that his sister suddenly came to the prison. She left me some tonic and 20 yuan, a lot of money in those days. I asked the guards to pass on my request that she not bring any more money again or anything else. But I was penniless in prison, so I kept 5 yuan and begged one of my wardens to send the rest to my mother. Of course I didn't know she was dead. This warden was a retired army officer. At first he refused, but I pleaded with him and he finally agreed. Later that sister-in-law sent another 30 yuan. She came five or six times altogether gave me about 120 yuan. Each time I asked the warden to send it on to my mother. Strangely, though, my family never wrote me even once about this. I thought maybe they just hated me too much. A year later, when I was sentenced, I was finally allowed to see them. Whenever they visited, wishing Chairman Mao longevity and studying his quotations would take up half of the time while the rest was filled with my sobbing. Not much chance to talk. My family didn't say anything about the money and it was too awkward for me to ask. It wasn't until 1979 when I was released that I discovered the money hadn't reached them. All those years I had regarded that warden as my benefactor. I still don't understand what was going on. Maybe the post office had refused to deliver the money since the postal service often refused to handle mail for families in disgrace. But even if that was the case, the money should have been returned to me.

Believe it or not, there were some decent prison workers. I had been quite healthy before, but now my weight had dropped to about forty kilos. A warden, seeing how thin I'd become, stealthily slipped my sister-in-law a health certificate.[3] The next time she came to visit, she was allowed to bring in a kilo of cakes. I was upset. I thought that it would be much better if the cakes had been given to my mother and nephews. Life outside was hard too. In prison I was given 1.50 yuan pocket money each month. I didn't buy anything except soap, toilet paper, and toothpaste, which would last me for months. I tried hard to save as much as possible. When I had saved 5 or 10 yuan, I'd send it home. For without my family's warmth, what did I have to live for? I tried my best under the circumstances to do something good for them. It was a kind of atonement.

In prison we also had to do political study and practice criticism. Very often I was called upon to denounce my crime of resisting the Cultural Revolution. Those in charge asked me to set an example of self-criticism at many meetings, both large and small. Self-criticism was really not so bad. Sometimes I'd be feeling very down. When it was my turn to self-criticize, I'd talk about the many years of education I'd received from the Party and how I should have believed in the Party and its policy. If I had followed the Party's policy, everything would have been all right. After each self-criticism session, my confidence in the Party would be reinforced and I'd feel better about going on living. I'd think about how to perform even better to get an early release and be able to pay back the Party. Believe it or not, good behavior did work. In 1972 my sentence was reduced from life to an additional ten years—the most lenient treatment I could have expected. I could get out in 1982. So I had something to hope for.

Not long after the Gang of Four was ousted in 1976, the courts reexamined my case. They decided that I had been persecuted during the Cultural Revolution. I was not a murderer, but rather a participant in a group suicide. Thus I was declared innocent and released. I got out in 1979, two and a half years earlier than I had expected. The new verdict went like this:

> The original sentence that Y committed the crime of murder in resistance to the Cultural Revolution is hereby declared invalid. Therefore the conviction is withdrawn and Y is declared innocent and is to be released.

I was released on the second of March, 1979. When I entered prison I only had on the hospital pajamas—the kind with blue and white stripes. Later, my brothers sent me a small suitcase of old clothes that I'd left with the rural medical team before the Cultural Revolution. I'd been wearing them for ten years. I was in rags when I came out. It was a heavy blow to learn that my mother had passed away a long time ago. It was my thoughts of her that had kept me going all those years. Now, with not only my father dead, but mother too, everything was finished. I was close to a nervous breakdown.

I came back home in March and started working in the Children's Hospital in May. I had had only two months rest. Lots of relatives and friends came to visit me. I couldn't sleep peacefully for all sorts of reasons. My mind kept going nonstop. I just couldn't relax. Three of us had planned to die together, but only I was alive. I felt terrible. People tried to comfort me, telling me how lucky I was even to be alive. So many higher-ups had followed Chairman Mao through hellish conditions on the Long March,[4] braving snow-covered mountains and impassable swamps. They too had been persecuted. Many had died; their families had been ruined. Their lot was worse than mine. But those who have survived are trying to make the best of things, aren't they?

My work unit was very considerate. When I was released, my family's houses were still occupied by others and hadn't been returned to us. So I just lived in the hospital dormitory. I'm a Muslim and my meals presented a bit of a problem. My nephew sent me suitable food every day by bicycle. He did this without fail for several years. As for my work, the hospital required me to work as a resident first. According to hospital regulations, you have to do a residency before getting an appointment as a staff doctor. I didn't have a home of my own to worry about, so I made full use of my time studying. In prison we weren't allowed to read professional books and journals so I had to double my efforts to make up for lost time. Before long, I got up to date.

I was put in charge of eight wards scattered between the first and fifth floors. Every day I ran up and down, fourteen hours a day. One night when I was on duty, I suddenly felt as though I was walking on clouds. I got someone to take my blood pressure. It was 180 over 100. Too high. I immediately asked for an injection. The one I got was supposed to be effective, but half an hour later it still hadn't worked. The systole was up to 200. The nurses decided among themselves to stop calling me for emergencies and let me rest. They were afraid I was exhausted. But I just continued my rounds. They were very sympathetic and showed their respect. What can I say? Well, I just doubled my efforts. Normally residency takes a full year, but in only six months I was promoted to staff.

Around this time I made a new acquaintance. He was a

graduate from the East China Textile Institute. When he was young, he had shown great promise and had been highly recommended by one of his colleagues, a chief engineer. During the "Antirightist" movement,[5] his mentor was denounced as a Rightist. My friend was asked to expose him. He refused. Instead he tipped off the engineer. To act against his conscience was not part of his character. He was treated as a Rightist and he himself believed that he was one. When the Rightists were delabeled, he was told that it had never been recorded in his files that he was one. The mistake was his own. But for twenty years he had believed this. He'd never gotten a promotion or raise. He hadn't even married for fear of the label. How could such an absurd thing have happened? When I met him he was over fifty and still single. Well, we got married. We have a lot in common and can communicate well. He's very considerate to me. We're a comfort to each other.

I adopted one of my brother's sons. He's studying a foreign language now in Beijing University. My husband was recently promoted to director of his factory. At last I have a real home and family.

Even today, though, I still can't rid myself of thoughts of the past. I don't think about it every day, but there's no escaping from my memories. In my mind my father's image appears again and again. My colleagues have asked me, "You couldn't even step on an ant, how could you have done it?" In the Cultural Revolution people were deprived of their basic humanity. Who in their right mind could stab their own father to death? Under normal circumstances no one would even consider it. And what about my mother? How can I make up for that? If I hadn't done what I did, my parents would perhaps be enjoying life today. If I'm not to blame, then who is? No matter how hard I try to justify my actions, I still fail. I can't decide whether I saved my father or destroyed him. In the beginning I felt that I had saved him but I feel more and more now that I destroyed him. Other things I can make sense of, but not this. My mind just goes round and round. All those bad things were caused by the Gang of Four. Why then did all those others survive until now and not my parents? It must be my fault alone. Whenever I think this way, I feel that I must have been guilty. It's too depressing. And yet my friends tell me that only when I enjoy life will my parents be able to rest in peace. They're right perhaps, aren't they?

I can't say any more. Please don't ask me to go on.

In dehumanizing times, the highest expression of human nature is destroying oneself. —F. J.

FOOTNOTES

1. The Military Control Commission of the People's Liberation Army replaced the police, the legal apparatus, and the People's Courts during the Cultural Revolution. It was given power to create laws and to put itself above laws.

2. A pocket-sized collection of Mao Zedong's best-known quotations. It has sold more copies than any book in history but the Bible. During the Cultural Revolution, every Chinese was supposed to have one, and often did.

3. A document showing that the carrier was in poor health and in need of extra nutrition.

4. The Long March was a major strategic movement of the Chinese Workers' and Peasants' Red Army, led by Mao Zedong, which succeeded in reaching the revolutionary base in northern Shaanxi after traversing eleven provinces and covering roughly 7,500 miles in 1934–1935.

5. In 1957 people who criticized the Party line were labeled Rightists. They were mostly intellectuals and were considered antisocialist reactionary elements.

A

T O U G H

G U Y

T I M E : *1966* ❦ A G E : *18* ❦ S E X : *Male*
O C C U P A T I O N : *Ordinary worker in a crane equipment factory in
T city.*

Well, to tell the truth, my family suffered pretty badly during those ten years. But I wasn't just some useless wimp. I was a pretty damn tough guy. Usually I'd take on anybody, but in those days even tough guys had to keep their heads down. But you've got to get out your feelings sometime, don't you? I've been holding mine inside for ten years. It's about time I found some release and that's why I'm here.

In 1966 I got through trade school and was assigned to work in a crane equipment factory. I was eighteen. Let me tell you about my family. I had parents, a grandma, two brothers, and a little sister. Grandma was eighty back then. Dad wasn't quite right in the head, not really out of his skull, but not all there either. My older brother had been strong as a bull, but he had a head injury from an accident at work and hadn't been normal ever since. My younger brother and sister were just little kids. So I was the only guy really capable of looking after the family. We were bad enough off to begin with. We sure as hell didn't need the Cultural Revolution.

I was worried from the start about what was in store for us. Because even though my family was pretty poor, we still supposedly didn't have the right class background. Before Liberation, my dad had worked as a traffic policeman for a year. Grandma's parents had some real estate and she and Grandpa became the managers. When they died, Dad took over. There were more than thirty apartments. In the 1950s, in the housing reconstruction period, ten of them were taken by the state. So Dad ended up as manager for about twenty rundown apartments. The "four cleanups"[1] didn't clear up our family status. We weren't counted as capitalists, but we weren't pure enough to be revolutionary working class either.

When the Cultural Revolution got started, houses were broken into and there was fighting everywhere. No one knew who'd be the next target. I once came across a whole clan, over twenty of them, lined up in the street. They had paper boards around their necks, and their hair was all cut short. You couldn't even tell the men from the women. All of them were being denounced in public by the Red Guards. I got really scared and ran home to sort out and burn everything those bastards might consider old.[2] I didn't want to look for trouble, right?

At first we lucked out. But when the "checkups"[3] started, everybody got investigated. One midnight some people came pounding at our door. They were the neighborhood committee

representatives with a bunch of local activists demanding to see
our residence cards. They searched our place and broke all sorts
of things. Pretty soon they came up with what they figured was
criminal evidence against my dad—his so-called restoration records.[4] It was only the accounts and receipts for the apartments,
but those idiots figured they'd struck gold. They dragged my
father to their neighborhood committee office and phoned his
work unit. His work unit people came that same night and
carted him away in a Jeep. They really believed that Dad kept
restoration records and was plotting to restore the old order.
What's the use of that stuff anyway and what in hell could
someone like my father do? He couldn't even talk right. He
had to get my little sister to write out his self-criticisms. A guy
like him was about to overthrow socialism? Bullshit! Chairman
Mao said, "Political power grows out of the barrel of a gun."
Dad wouldn't even have known which end goes bang. Well, he
still got locked up in the "cowshed." His crimes were being a
member of the KMT police and a reactionary householder. He
got denounced every day in all his factory's workshops, one by
one.

At this point the rest of us just shut ourselves up at home.
For days we didn't dare go out and get decent food or anything.
Grandma went nuts. The old girl was really terrified. She fell
one day and was paralyzed. She spent the rest of her days
suffering in bed till she died in 1972.

I went to Dad's work unit to try to explain his condition.
The guy in charge was a real SOB. He started yelling at me
even before I had a chance to introduce myself. "Why are you
sticking your nose into things?" he said. I figured that if I said
one more thing, I'd probably be accused of trying to restore the
old order too. And anything I said would make things worse
for Dad, so I just shut up and left. Really got pissed off.

Everything wrong got blamed on the Gang of Four, but

without a whole lot of other groups all over the place, how could they have done so much damage all by themselves? After my father got into trouble, my family's standing was shot. Overnight our neighbors started acting like they were better than us. The ones that had something or other against us weren't about to miss their chance. Everyone picks on you when you're down. We got shunned and cursed. Sometimes we'd even get a brick through our window while we were eating. Not a damn thing we dared to say or do about it. My mother got hit by a china jar thrown by a neighbor's kid. My fourteen-year-old brother was also hit over the head with a brick by another bastard and have to have nine stitches. His face was covered with blood. I couldn't even see his eyes, nose, and mouth.

We were human beings too. We couldn't put up with the insults and being picked on like this. So we went to the local Public Security Bureau to report. All they did was tell us we were "problematic" and we ended up having to apologize to our neighbors. No matter what we did, we were in the wrong. We were troublemakers because we dared to complain. I was a young man then and knew a little wrestling and kung fu. I had guts and was ready to fight for some justice. At another time I never would have put up with all that, but it was different then.

One night my older brother had a fit and was yelling and screaming. One of our neighbor's visiting country relatives came in and beat the hell out of him with a shoulder pole until he was rolling on the ground and was bleeding like crazy. Another neighbor finally stepped in and told that stupid farmer, "Stop beating him! He is a mental patient!" In spite of that some other bastard was yelling about how the "householder capitalist's" son deserved beating. It all happened while I was working the night shift. When I got home I saw clots of my brother's blood lying there on the ground looking like some rotten bean curd. I just about went out of my mind. I broke down and cried. I don't do that very often. I mean, you know, a man's not supposed to cry. But I couldn't help myself. I got so damn angry —I was breathing fire, the blood vessels on my neck were about to burst. I really wanted to beat the shit out of the bastards, but somehow I managed to hold myself back. I'm not stupid. If I did anything I'd be committing the crime of "class revenge" or some other crap like that. If they hung that rap on me, my dad and my whole family would really have been up the creek. I couldn't let that happen. It was pretty hard to swallow this one, but damn it, I did it.

These days I often think about what happened. My family was actually on pretty good terms with our neighbors. Never did anything bad to them or made any enemies. Why did they treat us so badly? Why did they change like that? It was all because of the goddamn Cultural Revolution!

I figured if I was going to make things any better for us, I'd better get politically progressive and work as hard as I could. So night and day I worked my ass off. I was in the team doing the hardest work. We had about twenty metal lathes and ran two shifts. The production quota was 240 hours a month each. No bonuses. I always managed to put in 300 hours, sometimes even 400. Aside from getting a drink of water or taking a leak, I stood by my lathe all day. Ten years of that. Never got there late or knocked off early. Not even a sick leave or anything. In the summer I worked bare-chested. We'd get red hot steel waste chips flying off the machines going everywhere, sometimes even into your eyes or on your skin. My lathe turned fast and had to be kept going all the time. Even when I got burned I kept on working. I finally convinced my coworkers that I was OK. I was given a bunch of model factory worker awards every year. I bet that if I worked like that now, I'd become a national model worker.

I made out OK at work but back home things were not easy.

My brother's brains got more and more scrambled because he was always getting picked on. He was just too crazy. Nobody could get any sleep. No hospital would take him because of our bad family status. Finally, he died at home.

My sister could have stayed in the city and worked[5] because our family was so poor. Even her school agreed. But politics got in the way and she was sent to the Inner Mongolian grasslands, a thousand miles away. Ninety percent of high school graduates with bad family status got sent there. Those who were considered all right went to the Great Northern Wilderness. My sister went through hell out there. She was really suffering from the climate, and the political pressures were pretty bad too. When she came back at twenty-seven after eleven years of that, she was totally wasted—her hair had even turned white. She only began to look normal again just lately. Can you imagine how I feel about it?

My father was now working as a boiler room janitor. After his shift he went around collecting the wasted coal bits to show his revolutionary conscience. He wouldn't get home until midnight. Some young pricks often took advantage of my dad's weirdness and would knock him around and throw him on the ground. He was mentally ill and even the constitution said he should be protected, but who gave a hoot about the law in those days? I couldn't stand my dad being treated like that. I wanted to find those guys and take them apart. But it wouldn't have done my family any good. Not a damn thing I could do.

Once a military unit came to my factory to recruit young people. To show my patriotism I wrote a letter in my own blood. It went something like this: "Resolutely vowing to safeguard Chairman Mao and the Party Central Committee and to defend our motherland to the death, I earnestly request to join the army." I figured that if I got to be a soldier, my family would be military dependents and their political status would get a lot better. I passed the physical and the army wanted me since I'd already shown myself to be a model worker. But again I got the boot because of our family background. The army just couldn't risk it. I didn't get anywhere that time either.

My factory leaders were touched by how hard I'd been working. They went to my father's factory over and over to try and sort out this family background business but got nowhere. We were stuck with this damn background crap for ten years. I lost a hell of a lot of weight and turned into a nervous wreck. Half of my stomach had to get cut out in an operation. Nothing worked. I just couldn't do anything to help my family. I felt so useless!

After the Gang of Four fell, my father was finally let off the hook. He was still the same guy as always but they no longer considered him "problematic." Shit! It's fucking absurd! I demanded that those bastards at his factory give him rehabilitation and compensation, but they told me the "cowshed" and the rest of the crap he went through was the fault of the "mass movement." He'd never officially been called a capitalist so there was nothing to rehabilitate him for. Those assholes just dismissed the whole thing with a few words. No worries for them. I really wanted to beat them to a pulp but a real man has to control himself. All right, even if you figured you were a tough guy, what the hell could you have done in that situation? So, that was my ten years.

Even a steel rod can be twisted into a question mark. —F. J.

FOOTNOTES

1. The "four cleanups," also called the Socialist Education movement, was a nationwide campaign to "clean things up" in the political, economic, organizational, and ideological spheres during 1963–1966.

2. At the beginning of the Cultural Revolution the Red Guards were searching out and destroying anything connected to the "four olds"—old ideas, old customs, old culture, and old habits.

3. Another national campaign begun in 1967 to single out landlords, rich peasants, reactionaries, evil elements, Rightists, spies, traitors, KMT remnants, and capitalist-roaders (a term often used during the Cultural Revolution for someone in power who followed the capitalist road).

4. Financial records supposedly kept by the former ruling class for possible future use in the event of a change of system.

5. If an urban family fell below a particular poverty line, all its members were allowed to remain in the city during the Going to the Countryside Movement.

A SENIOR RED GUARD'S APOLOGIA

TIME: *1966* 🦋 AGE: *20* 🦋 SEX: *Male*
OCCUPATION: *Student of a teacher's college in S city*

Before I came to see you, a few of my old pals who were also senior Red Guards said to me, "You go ahead and talk to him. Let him know about all the feelings we've kept inside." So here I am, not to give you a confession, but to tell you the way it was. I feel that until now we old Red Guards haven't been given a fair shake. If you've got the guts to get it all down, then I've got the guts to get it out. Of course, as you said, I'll have to start with my own experience—that's what it comes down to, experience. Is it OK, the way I talk?

I'm probably not going to get all this in the right sequence, but let me try. First I'll give you some background about what happened one or two years before the Cultural Revolution. I graduated from high school in 1964. My ambition then was to get into Nankai University in Tianjin to pursue my love of classical literature. But that year happened to be the prelude to the Cultural Revolution and those who went to the countryside were hailed as "pioneers." There was propaganda everywhere about Hou Jun, Xing Yangzhi, and Dong Jiangong.[1] I'd always believed in the Party and ever since primary school I'd been taught to follow the Party's directives without question. I have the proper working-class background. My father was a rickshaw driver and my mother was born and brought up in a peasant family. Before Liberation my parents had to sell one of my sisters as a servant to a big city capitalist just to make ends meet. My mother also worked for him as a wet nurse. Well, to make a long story short, the local government got my sister back after lots of trouble and effort. That's why I had such faith in the Party and had always followed it with total devotion.

However, something happened that cast a shadow of doubt over this devotion and really stuck in my mind. Back in 1954 when I was only in the second grade of primary school, I had a woman teacher named Miss Yan who taught me Chinese. Three years later she was labeled a Rightist. I was still too young to make any sense out of it. But I was extremely puzzled. She was really nice, so how could she become a Rightist? I went to see her again and she'd lost her sanity. When I got to her home, she wept in my arms. She said that she really wanted to yell at the top of her voice. Now I understand. She was branded a Rightist for speaking out and asking too many questions. You just couldn't do that. The Party leaders were the Party. They simply couldn't be challenged. The Party was infallible.

I've always followed the principle that whatever the Party says, goes for me. When I graduated from college in 1970 and had to fill out questionnaires to determine my future job assignment, I never wrote down my own preferences. Instead I simply stated that I would resolutely and willingly take any job the Party gave me. Looking back now, it seems that whoever toed the Party line ended up suffering, while those who refused to obey orders made out pretty well in the end.

Now, let's get back to the summer of '64. I suddenly decided not to take my college entrance exams but to go to the countryside instead. My family, of course, was strongly against it. Teacher Yan disagreed too, but she had to make a show of support. In those days who dared to openly oppose "going to the countryside?" You couldn't even just keep your mouth shut. Silence was the same as opposition. No matter what your feelings were, you were supposed to show enthusiasm. So, I went off to Baodi County in Hebei Province. There were seventy-one of us in all. We were really going all out for the revolution. Before we left there was a big farewell party and the mayor himself sent us off.

When we got there, the place was flooded. We had to be carried across the Hutuo River by the peasants. What we saw there wasn't what we had expected at all. Still, we were quite excited at first. We were still bubbling over with revolutionary zeal. But as time went by, life got pretty dull and grim. The hardest thing to take was hunger. We had to put up with just coarse wheat and corn flour and sometimes we even mixed in ground-up peanut shells when there wasn't enough to go around. No meat at all. Very hard to take. When I read in *Mimosa* about the starvation Zhang Yonglin[2] went through, I understood all too well. When you're starving, you're completely helpless. But even this didn't break my revolutionary spirit. Something happened, though, that even I couldn't handle.

Let me tell you about it. It was the time of the sorghum harvest in Baodi County. They plant it there between irrigation ditches. It had already been cut and bundled and since we were newcomers, we got stuck with the worst job: collecting the bundles. We had to trudge through those fields and ditches with the deep water and the sharp spikes of cut-off stalks everywhere. Pretty tiring and miserable work. Anyway, one day I went to the village teacher's house to borrow some books. I opened the door only to see some cadres there eating and drinking together. It was 1964. There was lots of propaganda about class struggle. People then were pretty simpleminded. We really had no idea what it was all about. We just saw all those villains in the propaganda films as class enemies.[3] Looking back now, those cadres had worked pretty hard too. All they had was a few scrambled eggs, some cold salad, and a big teacup of sweet potato liquor that they were all sharing. No big deal. But I was filled with the class struggle idea. Hey! What in hell were they doing? Those cadres were drinking and enjoying themselves behind the backs of the ordinary peasants! I thought it was outrageous. I couldn't contain myself and blurted out my feelings to my fellow workers. I was ignorant about the setup in that village. It had never occurred to me that everyone in the place was either named Sun—like the Party Secretary—or Jiang—like the Deputy Party Secretary: Everybody was related one way or another. So within a few days my words got around. One afternoon, after we returned from a day's work harvesting sorghum, the Party Secretary stood in the middle of the road cursing to the four winds.[4] The same night the Youth League Secretary, the Women's Committee head, and the rest of the cadres got together to denounce me. They listed my crimes: I wasn't following orders; I was trying to show off by taking on the complicated work . . . What did I know about those things?

66

What if I caused an accident or something? They kept going on and on in that vein. I was really caught in a predicament. I figured that there was no way I could stay there any longer.

Just at that time the "four cleanups" working team got around to our village. They were sent out to check on the local cadres and I immediately sided with them. But theirs were what you might call "rough cleanups." They only stayed for two months and then took off. I was left out in the cold again. I started to suffer badly. The Party Secretary ordered me to gather wheat. In this place they cleaned up the gleanings by hand for the second sowing. Really torture. I'd never done anything like that before. On top of it all, I had to work extra hours at night. Couldn't take any more. I started to think twice about my original dedication.

In the spring of '65 the State Council issued a circular promoting college admission for urban educated youths who had gone to the countryside. The commune leaders approached me and recommended me for admission. They said I only had to take the exams in Chinese and political studies.

I was only too happy to get out of that place. To my astonishment, the village leaders gave me a very decent report. I came across it later while I was ransacking my school's files during the Cultural Revolution. They wrote that I had deep feelings for the working class, had endured hardships, could stand up to hard work, and so on. A very good recommendation. Why did they do it? Well, they really didn't want me there. It was the villagers' way of getting rid of me. I realize now how good my luck was. If I hadn't gotten into trouble in the countryside, I never would have been able to go to college. Also, the people who got admitted in '65 were the last batch.

But perhaps my luck wasn't so great after all. I entered college in September 1965, and the Cultural Revolution started in

June the following year. The school was quite interested in me, an educated youth from the countryside. I was asked to take charge of student labor activities. My school was a new one, founded jointly by several big universities that contributed teachers and facilities. The first thing we studied was Wang Jie.[5] Any lessons? Well, in Modern Chinese Literature we only covered the *White-haired Girl*.[6] Oh yeah, we also studied the reportage on Dazhai.[7] Before we got to History, the "revolution" started, and from then on our studies took second place. Class struggle intensified. Well, I didn't care how much it intensified. I had a good family background and no obvious faults to pick on. Besides, I always followed the Party line, and I figured that as long as I followed the Party I had nothing to fear. Never tried to think things out before I acted, just acted automatically. How pious I was: I even kept a journal of all my activities, analyzing their ideological purity, emulating our model, Wang Jie. I kept the journal for my own edification, not like others who did it in the hope of getting published someday.

In my department some people hated me because I got along pretty well with some students who were from bad family backgrounds. But there was one guy from a really good background, a genuine poor peasant family for generations, who really got on my nerves. He couldn't be reasoned with. The year I spent in the countryside taught me that those poor peasants turned out to be the biggest troublemakers. The old rich peasants and landlords didn't dare stir anything up because they were already a thorn in the side of the masses. Since I wasn't crazy about my poor peasant classmate, I avoided him as much as I could. Some people tried to use this against me. One ideology instructor warned me not to hang out with the wrong type of friends and to watch which side I was on. I said, "What's wrong with them?" But talking back didn't do me much good. Another thing that caused problems was that I used to get up at 4:00 A.M. to go study in the empty classrooms. For this I got accused of being "white and expert."[8] Also I got on pretty good terms with the librarians so that I could borrow more books. I'd often go and help them with the cleaning up. I especially respected one librarian who had been labeled a Rightist in 1959. He was very knowledgeable and could even read *Selected Works of Mao Zedong* in English. This made yet another problem for me. But none of them would have mattered if it hadn't been for the Cultural Revolution.

That brings us to the Cultural Revolution. At the start we had no idea what was going on. It just came out of the blue, and the next thing you know people were acting like a mob. We were asked to expose and report on our department leaders. But what did we know about them? We'd only been there a few months. We really didn't have anything to say. But passivity wasn't the order of the day. If the Party urged us to put up big-character posters, we must do it. Until the editorial "Sweeping Away All the Monsters and Demons"[9] was published, I had only written one big-character poster on some trivial matter. Then the spirit of struggle intensified in the department. I'd be left behind if I didn't do something quickly. It was around the thirtieth of June. I put up another poster, this time about the person who was both head and Party Secretary of my department, accusing him of suppressing other teachers. This one turned out to be much more important than I thought.

Things began to get stickier. One day there was a report on a speech by a high official. The central theme was something like "revolutionaries fighting revolutionaries is a misunderstanding; revolutionaries fighting 'bad elements' is correct, and 'bad elements' fighting revolutionaries is insidious revenge...." The loudspeakers were blaring out that all Party members and

Youth Leaguers should attend a gathering. I was a Youth League member, so I raced down from the fourth floor to the auditorium. At the entrance were a fat woman with glasses from the Political Education department, a secretary, and the chairman of the student association. They barred me and others from entering, saying that we had to wait our turn. I'd always listened to what the Party said and figured they must have had a good reason for the delay. Surely they'd call us in later. So I left without saying anything, but on my way back to the classroom I began to wonder. Some of my college friends in Beijing had written me about the fast-developing revolutionary situation in the capital. They said that a lot of people had been singled out as targets of criticism. I had a bad feeling about this and didn't sleep a wink that night. The next day I decided to see the Party Secretary. He dismissed me with the excuse that he knew nothing about my situation. I was puzzled and also very angry, and decided to write another big-character poster about those people refusing to let me listen to the report. That same afternoon, when I was taking a nap, a student gofer was sent to tell me that I was summoned to the department head's office. I knew something was wrong. I rushed there with my heart in my throat. When I entered, the department head, deputy head, Deputy Party Branch Secretary, and political instructor, the work team sent to our department by the college Party committee and some other bigwigs, were sitting there. The scene sent chills down my spine. Back then students didn't dare visit the offices of big shots. It was just too far above us. This was the first time I had been there. I was so scared that everything seemed utterly unreal. They didn't offer me a seat, so I somehow found one. Extreme terror made me desperate. I asked them why they wanted me, something I'd normally be terrified to do.

A history teacher who was talented and a Korean War veteran replied, "Why don't you ask yourself that question?" I answered, "I wasn't allowed to listen to the report. I was deprived of my political rights." They all exchanged looks and changed the subject. Then the same teacher said, "We've learned that you've read *The Evening Chats at Yanshan*[10] and that you even took some notes." Well, that was true. I admitted it. He said, "Hah! You also discuss sex with the other students!" Well, they got me on that one too. I tried to remain calm and take the offensive. So I said, "But you're reading Jian Bozan;[11] how do you explain that?" The history teacher then replied, "Oh, that's a necessary part of my work. Don't you know that Deng Tuo is an antisocialist element? Shouldn't you examine yourself from that perspective?" "From what perspective?" I asked. The political instructor took over. "Examining whether one is anti-Party and antisocialist." I then said, "He should do that too."

Some others began lecturing me as well. They said that it's a good start to admit your errors. But there was more. "We heard that you once stated: 'Bourgeois of the world, unite,'" the political instructor said. "Don't you know how serious that is?" I especially remember that. She was very attractive, and a top-level graduate of a well-known university. Very sharp. At first, I couldn't figure out what she was talking about. So she told me: "You said it on a farm to a classmate." Then I remembered. When I was working on the school farm, a stupid classmate of mine kept asking me why all the books on Marxism began with the slogan "Workers of the World, Unite!" At that time I was young, about twenty or so, and quite arrogant. So I gave a lecture on the *Communist Manifesto*. Somehow my speech got reported to the school authorities and got twisted around. This was my second crime. The third one was this: They said that I wanted to be the school Party Secretary and cited the occasion they thought showed it. Again they got it all wrong. Our Party Secretary was really slack. One morning I saw him in the school garden fooling around shooting birds. I said something like being a Party Secretary must be a pretty easy job since he was obviously a man of leisure. The fourth charge against me was that I had stated: "It is right to rebel." Those stupid people didn't know that I was just quoting Chairman Mao. I'd heard from my Beijing friends that Chairman Mao had said, "The essence of Marxist principles in the final analysis can be summed up as it's 'right to rebel'." When this got published, the fourth charge was dropped. However the other three still stuck and I got labeled as one of the three reactionary students in our department. As for the other two, one got labeled because he had written a critical article about the mayor of Beijing. The other one came from a bourgeois family and indulged in his love of the bourgeois classical music of Tchaikovsky. So the three of us got listed: one an attacker of our proletarian leader, the mayor; one a descendent of the oppressors; and one, me, a working-class renegade.

From then on I was watched all the time. Even at night when I had to go to the bathroom, someone was posted there to keep an eye on me. I was so depressed that I cried many times when I was alone. What had I done against the Party? I thought I knew myself well, but I still put myself through the severest self-examination. One day I got a letter from my mother reminding me of our poor background and that I should always follow the Party unhesitantly, love Chairman Mao, and be active in the Cultural Revolution. She even sent me 20 yuan, which is a lot of money. I was really heartbroken. I couldn't let my mother know that I'd failed her and committed some serious errors. I got sick, too weak to even go to the dining hall.

Strangely enough, the department leaders got concerned and sent some students to persuade me to eat. I was really pissed off and told them that those leaders were the cause of my sickness in the first place. The department head came and said to me, "Your health has nothing to do with your problems. The Communist Party even treats captives well."

There was no reasoning with them. I couldn't do anything, so stuff it. I was young and strong and could support myself in any case. What really worried me was my family. What if they also thought I was anti-Party and turned against me too? I was going through mental torture. I even thought about committing suicide.

One day I went up to the top floor of our house where there was a balcony. There were posters everywhere. You could see as far as the city limits. I thought, If I just jumped, that would be the end of everything and I would be purified; on the other hand, if I jumped, then it would never be clear what had happened. I was deeply attached to my mother. She'd suffered in her life every kind of suffering that you could imagine. Back before the Liberation, she too had thought of killing herself, along with my second elder sister, when my parents were forced to sell her.

While I was thinking, a girl classmate came up the stairs and called out my name. I won't tell you her name. Her grandmother had been a maid for the Dowager Empress Cixi and her father a KMT member. So naturally she was an outcast. I had always shunned her before the Cultural Revolution. She sat behind me in class like a prissy high-class lady—at least, that's how I saw her. And she was always very forward toward men. I was twenty then and she was eighteen.

I asked her, "Why did you follow me?" She in turn asked me, "What are you doing here?" She added, "I heard you were sick." I remarked, "Yeah, and you're the only one who didn't come to see me." Then she said something I'll never forget: "I don't really feel you are a bad person."

That she could say this to me under the circumstances really overwhelmed me. At that time no one talked to me, especially my close friends. Before all of this, eight of us would sit together at dinner and share four big dishes. But now they all shunned me.

I replied, "You must be kidding." She said, "I never lie to anyone. What kind of person do you think I am? I know you look down at me." To tell you the truth, she was really beautiful. What she said made me—how do I say it?—feel warm inside.

So I asked her, "Are you free tomorrow? I'd like to go somewhere." She asked me where, but I said, "Maybe you'll be afraid to go." She answered, "There isn't any place I'm afraid of." I suggested Dr. Bethune's [12] cemetery. "But how can you get away with so many watchdogs around you?" she asked. "And why go there? Do you want to worship at his tomb?" I replied, "How can you talk like that about the great martyr?" Though she was very nice to me, our ways of thinking were on different tracks. We went there anyway the next day. She wasn't afraid of anything. We fell in love.

She once said, "From now on you're tied to me, the daughter of a former KMT member." I said, "What's it matter anyhow? It's all screwed up as it is. The Communists don't want me anymore. More problems won't make any difference." I don't really know why she loved me. I guess we were just friends in need, sharing our misery. Looking back, I'd say she was after some sort of fairy-tale romance. Maybe. Maybe not. But I do know that if not for her, I would have been much worse off. Her courage moved me, and we had this strong bond between us. No matter how much I was criticized, it didn't mean a thing. I was no longer alone. I felt like I was part of a great cause.

One day we were sitting in the forest behind Dr. Bethune's cemetery. I said, "I never expected you to be so kind." She said, "Don't mention it. I'm nobody. I've lived with my KMT label for so many years." I didn't know what to say. But in high school, before the Cultural Revolution, I had read quite a lot of foreign literature, and so I had some idea of romance. I feel now that it was the only time I was really in love. I was quite naive back then and felt she would be mine forever and nothing would ever change.

So that's how the Cultural Revolution began for me: When I was almost ready to kill myself I found my first love. I'll never forget her. Never.

I was sent to the school farm to do hard labor along with some Rightists, opportunists, former KMT officers, deviationists, and so on. The students in Beijing had already begun a criticism movement against their teachers, but in our area things were moving more slowly.

It was August. The peanuts and sweet potatoes were getting ripe. I had this sudden urge to get close to old Rightists, I'm still not sure why. One night I snuck out to visit a former librarian. He'd been given a place next to the pigsty and was still reading Mao's works in English. Frankly, in those days I couldn't really make myself hate the Rightists, and even when the librarian warned me that he'd been labeled, I insisted that that's why I came. I said, "Rightists are human beings too. Why can't I associate with them?" I started to chat with him about my own problems, but he just sat there and refused to talk. I came back the next day and got the same response. But the third day was different. He opened up a little. I had told him that I wanted to learn from him, but he quickly cut me off with the statement, "I'm guilty...." I pressed him. I said I wanted to know how to avoid making ideological mistakes. He stared at me for a while and then said, "Well, since you enjoy reading, there's a way." At the time his words sounded like some sort of Buddhist allegory. He went on. "If you have a favorite book, that book must be problematic, because we have so many bourgeois and revisionist ideas in our minds. Find a book or a section of a book that you really like, then write a condemnation of it —and you'll never go wrong." I took his words as gospel and they proved to be very effective.

At that time every policy had to follow the editorials in the Party publications. Afterward Mao's quotations became our sole bible. On the tenth of August, 1966, we all were summoned to listen to an important broadcast about the Sixteen-Point Directive.[13] It expressed exactly what I felt. I can still clearly remember the announcer's loud, resonant, and militant voice. So different from today. Some sentences went like this: "During the present struggle the orientation of our youth has been basically correct. Even though they may have made some mistakes, it is imperative to prevent people from categorizing them as counterrevolutionaries. It is also necessary to guard against political opportunists. The main objective of the struggle is to defeat and crush those in power within the Party who are pursuing the capitalist road...." To tell the truth, these words really struck home. My adoration of Chairman Mao became deeper than ever before.

Immediately after the broadcast we rebelled against the school farm authorities. I alone went back to the school, walking the 20 km or so. It wasn't easy in the darkness. No one else in sight. Just trudging along the bumpy fields next to the river. However, I was too excited to care. As soon as I got to the school I lost no time in stirring up the other students. I made friends with a guy from the Political Science department who'd had an experience similar to mine. I encouraged him. "Let's rebel," I said. "Can't you see what's going on?" I felt that I thoroughly understood the Party's policy. That evening, along with students from the Mechanical Engineering department, we formed an organization of our own. We hung up a big-character poster from the fourth-floor window. On it was written the much quoted slogan "He who does not fear being cut to pieces dares to unhorse the counterrevolutionary cabal."

That night I wrote another poster entitled "My Persecution by the department head." It was five o'clock in the morning when I finished putting it up. I was exhausted, so I lay down on the Ping-Pong table, with ink and paste all over me, an exquisite sense of relief and emancipation flooding through my body. I had just listed the facts, what they did to me, when, and so on, and put up the poster in an inconspicuous place, yet it got an enormous response. Everybody had listened to the Sixteen-Point Directive as of course they had to and the next day all hell broke loose. People who had previously sympathized with me in silence began to openly voice their support. I wished I knew some tactics for uniting people like the old revolutionaries, but instead I reasoned that they should have shown me support earlier. So to hell with them. The only kinds of comrades-in-arms I needed were like my first girlfriend. She rushed to see me while I was resting after putting up the poster. We hugged each other and were both wild with joy. I was politically liberated! A genuine revolutionary and an innovator too! All my past fears were forgotten.

My poster turned my department upside down. Posters of solidarity covered the school like snowflakes. Surprisingly, even those Leftists who had caused me so much trouble before also expressed their support. I hated that student association Chairman and the Communist Youth League secretary the most. Sometimes I could be pretty arrogant, and I said to them, "Now see who laughs last!" I demanded that a meeting be held to show that my ideology was purer than that of my former persecutors. It didn't occur to us then to single out the department leaders. Really, I'm a humane person. As long as I saw justice done, I didn't want to push it too far, especially when I saw my department head with his head already sunk so low. Fair is fair. To my astonishment, everyone in the school showed up at the meeting, even without any formal notification.

The meeting was held in the auditorium. No set agenda. The Youth League secretary presided. Even we rebels didn't dare attempt to get rid of him and still felt he should be in charge at that juncture. Our minds were too shackled to overtly challenge authority. We didn't go to the platform either, just set up some temporary tables and a microphone. I spoke first, telling the story of my persecution. I was really scared speaking in front of that huge crowd. It was August twelfth, very hot and stuffy. The more I spoke, the worse I felt. I had been so unjustly treated and all the other sad things in my life kept crossing my mind too. I just couldn't help crying. It wasn't an act and the effect was quite powerful. The audience was really getting indignant. Emboldened by the Sixteen-Point Directive, they started to chant slogans like "We strongly protest the persecuting of a young revolutionary by the comrade department head." Gradually even "comrade" was dropped and things got nastier and nastier. The opposition was angry too and tried to sabotage us by turning off the loudspeakers. That was the worst thing they could have done. How dare they try to silence us! My department's students were pretty passive, but before I could do anything the engineering students were on their feet and smashing windows everywhere. You see, mass movements are often not orchestrated. They just happen.

By now the revolutionary momentum in the school was reaching its climax. That same night we rebels announced that we had occupied the school broadcasting room. We also issued a directive demanding that the school Party secretary and his deputies immediately come to the auditorium. Now we were fearless. Before we didn't even dare address the Party secretary by name, but now we were ordering him around. However, the Party secretary and the other leaders were wily old foxes. They were afraid that the students might give them a good beating, so they laid low. In fact we didn't have the guts yet to try that. You could characterize our revolt as something like rebelling while still bending the knee. All we were after was for them to express support for us. Really, that's all. But instead they refused to show up and aborted our meeting. So next a group of us forced our way into the school Party committee office. We'd never even dared to go there before, but this time we compared ourselves to the peasants of the twenties rising up against the evil landlords. When we got in we were bowled over by the luxury. Sofas everywhere, common now, but real status symbols back then. That threw us off a bit. The Party secretary, a skinny old man, asked us what we wanted. We students in front were pretty nervous and hesitant, but the ones in back pushed us forward. I got criticized later for not being a total rebel in the examination of class struggle behavior, but I really couldn't bring myself to attack that Party secretary. To me he still represented the Party. But then he opened the confrontation with what amounted to a dismissal. "Oh, I don't know anything about your problem," he said. This really annoyed me, so I said, "OK, since you don't know anything, you take your people to the auditorium and find out what's what."

When the Party people finally left, the office was at our mercy. We all plumped ourselves down on the sofas. We weren't going to miss that chance. We turned the place into the temporary headquarters of our Cultural Revolution committee. I thought that would be the end of it, but I still hadn't figured out what the movement was all about. It was only the beginning. Our school, as I told you, was jointly set up by different institutions. There were several main strands among the teachers and staff—some there for on-the-job training, some from the polytechnics, some from the teachers' colleges—as well as a group of volunteers from all over the country. The cadres from the different places all had their own toadies. So what we had done was like throwing a stick of dynamite among them. Because they knew each other so well, we had set off a chain reaction of counteraccusations.

On the eighteenth of August Chairman Mao reviewed the great public assemblies of Red Guards. The struggle in my school had accelerated. We had joined the forefront of the revolutionary Leftists and we began to actively denounce our school leaders. I now understand what was really happening. Our student movement got mixed up with the staff's factional conflicts. We were used as pawns. You had to follow along when revolutionary struggle was forging ahead. And once you got involved, you couldn't back off. But as time went by I started to get fed up with the violent fighting. It was getting out of hand. I myself never beat up anyone during the Cultural Revolution, although it's probably useless to tell you that now. One thing that I found pretty remarkable was that those people who were supposedly conservative bootlickers turned out to be the most brutal once they decided to join the rebellion. To them, beating up others was a way of demonstrating their revolutionary zeal. I'm not sure whether you like hearing that or not, but that's the way it was.

I still remember the scene when we denounced my department head. He'd treated me badly before but was quite apologetic later. I also learned that he was a veteran revolutionary cadre who had joined the Party in 1938. He was a scholar too, specializing in Lu Xun's [14] essays. I also admired his scholarship. I worshiped learned people like that. How could I hate him, let alone beat him? Once during a criticism meeting he was forced to wear a dunce cap. The thing was made from a wastepaper basket with paper glued around it. I'd run out of new criticisms, but the others would get ticked off if you just repeated the same old stuff. So I had to come up with something "from a higher plane of principle," as we said in those days. Even I felt that my criticisms weren't too convincing. The head was over fifty and had high blood pressure and stuff like that. As we were denouncing him, he was told to turn around in circles on a chair with his dunce cap on. You didn't dare show any sympathy in such an atmosphere. I left the moment I finished my speech. I didn't have the heart to torture him, but you had to put on a good show. The harsher you were, the more revolutionary you'd be considered. That's why things got so bad. For example, there was this girl student from my own class, a Youth League branch secretary. She had long clawlike fingernails and used them on the department head's scalp. There were gashes and blood all over him. The sight really revolted me. I'm not trying to defend myself but damn it, I have human feelings too. Ah, what's the use of telling you this? I know what kind of person I am.

Afterward I went to see the department head. He was sitting there sobbing to himself. I had to keep up my revolutionary front, so I sternly told him to confess any faults he might have. I continued, "Of course we'll stick to the facts about you. We won't allow any fabrications." I was using harsh officialese, but I was trying to convey my compassion for him. The head said

to me, "If your genuine purpose is to criticize me, then I will
offer no resistance. But the way you're going about it is more
than I'm able to bear." It really made me sad. I paused for a
moment, then asked him to take out his "Little Red Book."
"OK," I said, "you turn to this page. Remind yourself of the
quotation 'We should trust the masses and we should trust the
Party. With these wise revolutionary principles, no problems
are too difficult to overcome'." That was all I could come up
with and yet it comforted him. He understood me. That's why,
years later when I finally graduated from the college, and when
he was finally "liberated," he invited me to dinner to show his
appreciation. For a department head to do this for an ordinary
student is almost unheard of.

By the end of August we'd started to travel all over the
country to exchange revolutionary experiences. Even now, I
don't have any regrets. That travel experience was the best I've
had in my life. We first traveled to Beijing, then Yanan, Wuhan,
and even Aksu in southern Xinjiang. From Beijing to Yanan
we went on foot just like the revolutionaries had done in the
Long March. All together we spent about twenty days on the
road. We enjoyed the landscape enormously, much too excited
to even feel tired. We sometimes covered as much as 40 km a
day, but usually only managed 25 km.

At our first stop, Beijing, we had free food, thanks to Vice-
Premier Comrade Tao Zhu.[15] I can still remember stewing pork
and potatoes in a huge barrel with rice to follow. You could eat
as much as you wanted. Sleeping was a bit of a problem. Classroom floors strewn with straw were our beds, but no one complained. We were there for the revolution.

I had two things in mind when I came to Beijing. The first
was to actually see Chairman Mao, Vice-Chairman Lin Biao,
and comrade Jiang Qing. The second was to investigate the

situation at the Beijing Writer's Association. I got to see Chairman Mao three times. The first time I was really excited. We were up most of the night at Qinghua University before setting out for Tiananmen Square. People were pretty disciplined and conscientious back then. It was very easy to organize things and those few hooligans or thieves who were around were probably lying low because of the tense atmosphere. The "dictatorship by the masses" was formidable: All you had to do was come up with a quote from Mao and everyone would toe the line. All over China people were watching each other. If you yawned in Shanghai, they'd hear you in Beijing. Anyhow, people were a lot easier to control than now.

On the thirty-first of August I saw Chairman Mao. About three o'clock in the morning, we were awakened by blaring loudspeakers calling for people from each province to assemble at different places. In a confused rush we just grabbed anything we could find to wear—mostly old-style tattered military uniforms like the veteran revolutionaries had worn. We set out for Tiananmen but had to wait at Xinhuamen[16] to enter the square. I was told that I was one of the group representatives from Hebei Province to sit in the reviewing stand under the Tiananmen rostrum,[17] though it turned out I would have been better off on Changan avenue, since this time Chairman Mao chose to descend to the road and walk across Jinshuiqiao before getting into a car that drove through the crowds, letting us all have a real glimpse of our Chairman.

We ended up waiting for this until three in the afternoon, but we didn't even think about food. Luckily, though, some people sent us baskets of bread plastered with slogans like "Saluting the Red Guards from all over the country." I still even remember what type, one of those long thin loaves. I just stuck it in my pocket and nibbled a bit from time to time. I remember too a young girl, a southerner from Jiangsu Province. I've always liked southerners and we chatted the time away. Finally Chairman Mao appeared. You could have heard a pin drop; everyone was so awed. Can you imagine a place like Tiananmen Square with millions of people suddenly as silent as a tomb?

Well, that silence lasted a few seconds. When Chairman Mao crossed Jinshuiqiao, pandemonium broke out. Everyone was cheering and crying at the same time. That southern girl was too short to see anything with all the people pushing and shoving to get a better view, but I was pretty strong and managed to get to the front for a good look. Mao was in fine shape. His face shone with health and vigor. How marvelous a figure was our leader! But when we saw Lin Biao just behind him, we were shocked. How could our Vice-Chairman be so skinny? That's what kept running through my mind. Later on I told my mother about it and we worried that old skinny Lin could never survive Mao to be his successor.[18]

Anyhow, back to my story. That little southern girl was really upset because she couldn't see anything. I offered to help her and she asked me to lift her up. We were very innocent. Even though she was my own age, the thought of sex never occurred to us. When I lifted her she was wild with joy shouting over and over, "I see him! I see him! . . ." She got so excited she even dropped her "Little Red Book" somewhere in the crowd. Mao's convertible drove slowly around Tiananmen Square for ten minutes with the crowd shouting themselves hoarse. This was the first and longest time that I saw the Chairman. I saw him again on the fifteenth of September that year and a third time maybe in October. I can't remember the date.

I also got to hear Mao's wife Jiang Qing. I was honestly inspired by what she had to say, though her tone of voice was a bit weird. Just like those imitations the stand-up comics did after her downfall. Hearing her reinforced my ambition to rebel. I felt as though I was justified in doing anything—things I didn't even dare dream of before. That's one of the things that came out of that trip.

The experience of traveling also started me thinking about lots of things. I went to the Beijing branch of the Writer's Association. Big-character posters were everywhere, denouncing everybody, even people like Mao Dun [19] and Du Pengcheng.[20] They said Mao Dun kept many servants and young nurses at home to wait on him. He was characterized as a leech sucking the blood of the people. Many things I had thought sacred before were instantly shattered. I also witnessed the denunciation of Tian Han [21] in the backyard of the Association compound. I respected Tian Han the most and enjoyed his plays enormously. What I saw was horrifying. Tian's hair was shorn to the roots just like a monk's. He had a big cardboard placard hung around his head denouncing him as a counterrevolutionary revisionist element. Getting punished next to him were also two famous writers of the Folk Literature Research Institute, Jia Zhi and Ah Jia. Techniques of humiliation were much more advanced in Beijing than elsewhere. Tian Han was forced to sit on his knees with his head virtually pushed to the ground. On his scalp you could see three bloody razor tracks where they must have just finished shaving him and he didn't even have much hair to start with. The guys torturing him looked like some sort of cadres, mostly in their forties and fifties. Not us Red Guards. Tian's "crimes," all listed, were mostly private and trivial matters. During the Cultural Revolution they always mixed serious political offenses with personal stuff. As you well know, we Chinese always like to stick our noses in each other's private lives. If you only picked on how he'd pursued the revisionist road and advocated counterrevolutionary ideas, people would get bored. But some good tidbits of personal gossip could make you instantly infamous, and of course, your political standing would go down the drain. That's how it worked.

When we were gallivanting around the country, travel by rail was free. The trains were packed; even the toilets were full of people. Some got themselves a place by lying on the overhead luggage racks. If you actually had a seat you didn't dare to move. I remember one girl from Hunan. She sat next to me for three days without moving or eating anything. She was afraid she'd lose her seat if she left. Soon as we got to a stop and the doors opened, huge crowds would fight their way in. People were sleeping all over the place. Incredible maybe, but believe it or not, we were really happy.

When we traveled from Shanxi Province to Shaanxi Province, we lost some of our exuberance when we saw the poverty-stricken villagers everywhere. In one place a little boy wanted to trade all the herbal medicine he'd gathered that day for my Mao badge. Tears welled up in my eyes. I reckoned it was the deep love of our people for Chairman Mao. I didn't accept the herbs of course. No use anyway. I quickly took off my badge, collected several other shapes from my classmates, and gave them all to the kid. He accepted them as if they were treasures. His mother told him not to play with them but to worship them. In the rural areas people used to hang up a picture of the kitchen god. Now they worshiped Mao's portrait in its place. They idolized him literally, turning Mao into a deity figure. Thinking about it now, it was a real tragedy.

When we got to Yanan[22] we were even more disappointed. The place was just a huge muddy hill. Nothing at all attractive. The famous pagoda there was a mess and the northern Shaanxi people were nothing like what we had expected. The towels they used to tie around their heads were just filthy rags. They didn't resemble the carefree and happy people depicted in the dances shown on stage at all. They were indifferent to us Red Guards. We put ourselves up in the local Red Guard reception center. It was already filled with other travelers. There wasn't anything there except a photo of Mao and Jiang Qing with their children. I started to wonder after the trip, what kind of a revolution is this? People were still so poor. In the village I just mentioned some young girls were going about with pants full of holes. Why did the Chinese people have to live so badly? I felt very depressed. Yanan was the revolutionary crucible—the first stronghold of the Communist Party. How could it still be so poor?

By November 1966 everyone had returned from their travels. All had learned something in their own way. Different factions were consolidating their forces and lots of denunciations were going on. The school's struggle had integrated with society's. There were mainly two factions now, divided by their attitudes toward the PLA soldiers becoming part of the leadership of civilian organizations. The organization I belonged to was promilitary. The opposition faction was putting up lots of anti-military posters. So every night, even in the freezing cold, we'd go out on patrol wearing our hard hats with a cart full of glue bottles and poster paper. When we found their posters, we'd stealthily cover them over and write new slogans like "Resolutely Support the PLA" and "Those Who Want to Undermine the 'Great Wall of Steel'[23] Will Have Their Dog Turd Skulls Smashed." You should know. We were very serious. I felt that no matter what, you just couldn't oppose the PLA. After all, it was they who liberated all of China. To me they were saints.

At the time there were lots of civilian fighting corps all named after Chairman Mao's poetry. Some of the names were like "Rebelling-to-the-End" corps, "Smiling-Amidst-Flowers" corps, "Stern-Face-to-the Pacific" corps, and so on. There was even one group called the "Madmen Rebellion" corps. They all had their names written on red armbands and each group had its own strict code of discipline. I often saw dead bodies being carried through the streets by the "Madmen" after faction fighting. Once we got word that one of the fighting corps was attacking a military office. We immediately got together about a thousand people—easy to do then—and ran to protect them.

At this time I was in charge of observing the development of the movement and keeping in touch with other units around the country. All the written propaganda was checked by me. Sometimes I'd go out into the streets to have open debates with other factions. About ten loudspeakers would be mounted on a truck. Our announcers were really good, much better than those found nowadays. My girlfriend was one of them. Her voice was incredible. She could go on nonstop for five hours. The announcers didn't use any prepared texts, yet still they sounded very logical and convincing. We had also trained a person who specialized in reciting quotations from Marx, Engels, Lenin, and of course Mao. As soon as you needed one, this guy could come up with a quote exactly appropriate for the occasion. He was a physics major and had a very good memory. Just knowing Mao's works was no big deal. Even I could recite by rote Mao's third volume, *The Three Articles*. We had nothing else to read anyway. But this guy could recite even the most obscure stuff. We called him the "Marxism-Leninism Ammunition Depot."

Getting back to our fight to protect the military office, we were beaten up by the other side. They outnumbered us and we had to retreat. With workers in the vanguard, they pushed past us toward the soldiers. We knelt down in front of them and I cried out, "How can you workers fight against the PLA? Without the PLA where would you be?" A few of the older workers hesitated but the rest rushed on. At this point some soldiers came out, all carrying their "Little Red Book." They got beaten up pretty badly. I witnessed with my own eyes how the PLA soldiers took the beating without lifting a finger in their own defense. They were slapped repeatedly in the face but stoically held their hands in front of their chests to show they wouldn't fight back. The soldiers were black and blue from the beatings, with swollen lips and bleeding noses. I eventually found out that they were told to do this beforehand in case pictures were taken that could be used against them later. Things weren't as simple as we thought. Even the PLA was manipulated by others, but at the time I was moved to tears by their bravery. After this violent episode our school struggles became entangled with the mass struggles going on throughout society.

Large-scale violence occurred mainly in the summer of '67. The worst of it was in Sichuan Province, where artillery and fighter planes were mobilized. Our province probably came second. At first people only used their fists and feet, but things got rougher later. I was once a member of a fighting group. The two factions in the school each occupied a building. Lots of damage was done. We smashed the windows of our own building with iron bars for fear our opponents might throw stuff at us and we'd get hit with flying glass. We also knocked down the wooden stairs and used movable ladders instead. We had no provisions so we seized and looted passing food trucks. Sometimes some of the drivers would be sympathetic to our cause and park near our building on purpose so we could steal their goods.

Once I broke my leg during a fight, and PLA soldiers sent me all the way to Norman Bethune International Hospital in the city. Crowds of Little Red Guards[24] came to salute me with bunches of flowers, though I wasn't exactly injured in action.

Some of the Red Guard girls were really courageous. During the fighting we would all throw stones at each other. In the lulls, the girls would run out to the middle of the "battlefield" carrying sacks on their backs to collect our stone "bullets." I am nearsighted and not a good fighter, so I concentrated on my special field of getting information from the other side. Most of our spies among them were won over by the tactic of sowing discord, that is, inciting them against their leaders. Money didn't come into it because we didn't have any to bribe them with. Who had money in those days? For example, we'd pass word to a veteran rebel that he should long ago have been promoted to an "odd-job man" instead of remaining a small-potatoes ordinary fighter. "Odd-job man" was what we called cadres in those days, following the no-title principles of the Paris Commune.[25] Well, that old boy would get pretty disgruntled and maybe become a spy for us. We also used disinformation, sending our people to join the other side and give them false intelligence. That was our fifth column. Our opponents had a four-member "Cheka"[26] to ferret out our agents. Those caught were given severe beatings. We did the same thing of course. Once we caught a girl spy—a chemistry student, real frail-looking with glasses. We locked her up in a small room and one of our girls, a big strong girl from Handan, beat her with a leather belt. But that other girl was fearless and steadfast. The leather strap was strong and wide. Within minutes her face and arms were covered with blood, but she still stuck to her convictions. She said she wouldn't change her allegiance even if we beat her to death.

I honestly think that over 90 percent of the Red Guards were deadly serious about carrying out the revolution. I remember one girl student from the Teacher's University. She told me that she felt like one of the comrades defending the Paris Commune.

Once, different factions were shooting at each other with small-bore rifles. Some started retreating, but she resolutely advanced and caught a fatal bullet in the head. Think about it: If she had any selfish motives, would she have done that? When I talk about the Cultural Revolution, I don't feel any remorse. I can confess what we did, but no regrets. When we joined the movement we had no ulterior motives. We were dedicated and we suffered for it too. Once the real violence got under way, we didn't dare close our eyes or even undress at night. One whistle blow and we'd be instantly on our feet. Day and night meant nothing. To retreat an inch would be total humiliation. There were some people who stayed out of things and didn't take sides. But as far as we were concerned, they were worse than dog shit. It's not fair to put all the blame for what happened on us Red Guards. The Cultural Revolution was simply a policy misdirection. It was like the "Fifth Antiencirclement" campaign in Jingangshan.[27] You can't blame the Red Army soldiers, can you? Were their deaths worthless? In a war, when the commander makes mistakes, the common soldiers are still martyrs. Aren't they?

When the violence escalated in June 1967, it became an armed conflict. We were told that our enemies had already armed themselves, so of course we had to do so too. Comrade Jiang Qing exhorted us to use "verbal attack and armed defense." What's defense without guns? We decided to seize them from the PLA. Actually it wasn't much of a seizure as the PLA was quite cooperative. When we went to the PLA armory, the doors were wide open and not a soul was in sight except for the guard. He even led us through the storeroom with his flashlight, asking us what stuff we wanted. We got the weapons but had no idea how to use them. In our target practice I could never hit the target so I didn't even get the chance to use my gun.

In my opinion it was Chairman Mao who initiated the Cultural Revolution, but in the later years not even he could control the situation. In the beginning people plunged into the movement of their own accord. They were sincerely and piously following our Great Leader both to carry out our revolution against revisionism and to preempt any further revisionism. But our idealism went downhill when the riots began all over the country, especially in Shanghai. Some people quickly realized which way the wind was blowing and took advantage of the situation. That's when things started to get dirty. When anyone got a little power, their personal interests took over. Even within the Party the factional strife was obvious. Political opportunists seized the chance to gain control. You could describe the beginnings of the Cultural Revolution as a sacred movement, but later it degenerated into a vicious power struggle.

In November 1967 our school's revolutionary committee was set up, the first in the province. Soon the provincial revolutionary committee was also established. On both occasions I drafted a letter of congratulations. The committee was called "three-in-one" as it consisted of workers, PLA, and Red Guards. It resulted from a redistribution of power, and naturally with it came a struggle for more power. In the vanguard were the Red Guards. The PLA and workers came in second and third. The PLA had supported us and we thought of them as our saviors. But when the Mao Zedong Thought Workers' Propaganda Team[28] entered the school in 1969, we Red Guards lost all status and were treated like so much crap.

Another thing that upset us was that in 1968 academic studies were still not permitted. We felt that the Cultural Revolution was drawing to an end and it was time to get back to school. So we demanded a "resumption of classes while carrying out the revolution." The PLA Propaganda Teams, who by then had taken control, told us we could only resume "classes" in Mao Zedong thought" and "Applied Marxist Dialectics," that is, continual mass criticism meetings. Academic studies? Even the word was anathema. We should study "Skills to Serve the People." At this point an editorial was published advocating extreme leftist ideas in education. I was a veteran rebel. Together with another two fellow rebels and the help of that "Marxism-Leninism Ammunition Depot," we put up a wall poster entitled "Questioning the March Second Editorial." We stuck it up just outside the news agency office. The same day many wall posters appeared attacking us. Several truckloads of people came to the school, challenging us to debate. The PLA representative lectured me. "Rebels should always make new contributions," he said, "but Chairman Mao has now stated that the Red Guards have begun making mistakes." As a result I was deserted by the school and left to the mobs. I was only spared because a few former rebel comrades-in-arms protected me. From then on I withdrew from all political organizations and had bad relations with the school.

I joined the school literary group to write plays. One was called "Spring Arrives at the Great Wall." The gist of it was this: A capitalist-roader[29] factory director badly persecutes the workers and falls under the attack of the masses in the Cultural Revolution. The factory is ideologically purified and progresses in the right direction. Back then, of course, all literary works followed the same pattern.

The school didn't calm down. One campaign after another. One was called the Campaign Against the Three Anti-Elements.[30] A schoolmate, having nothing else to do, wrote a slogan on the window ledge reading something like, "A sea voyage depends on the helmsman and carrying out the revolution depends on...." Before he had finished writing the final words, ". . . Mao Zedong thought," he was called away to do something. The words were partially erased but you could still read them. Someone else, God knows who, finished it with ". . . the biggest contemporary revisionist." A girl student spotted it and shouted frantically, "A counterrevolutionary slogan! A counterrevolutionary slogan!" People panicked and reported it. The guy got arrested. He was my roommate for two years. How could he suddenly become a counterrevolutionary? Meeting after meeting was held in every department to criticize him. The military representative shouted, "Class struggle has now entered our very midst! You must be merciless even with your friends and kin. That's the essence of Marxism." That was nonsense. I didn't dare to speak out, though, as I'd be singled out as a "bad element" too. Other students volunteered to expose my roommate's "crimes." What the hell did they know about him?

Around 1968 the Red Guards themselves began to be the target of revolution. That roommate of mine was sentenced to ten years in prison and paraded in humiliation all over the city. Another one suffered a similar fate. When he had finished writing a wall poster, he rinsed his brush and, shaking it dry, inadvertently splashed some inky drops on a Mao portrait. He didn't dare burn it so he quickly folded it up and hid it under his blanket. He then just forgot about it. One day the school distributed pesticide to the students for killing bedbugs and the damaged portrait was discovered. The PLA soldiers were truly merciless. They arrested him on the spot and he also got ten years. It was really scary, even worse than the white terror[31] before Liberation.

I was fed up with all the fighting, criticism sessions, and constant tension. So much of it from selfish motives. So you see, even then I showed a better conscience. Right? Another thing was that I was getting old and facing graduation. Most of us felt enough was enough. My first girlfriend left me, probably because I was too unstable. Later, I found another girlfriend. She was the daughter of a revolutionary martyr, and big and strong. She told me she worshiped me. In those days girls behaved like men. If they acted like ladies, they must be bourgeois decadents. They used vulgar language and went around with their sleeves rolled up. That was the right way to be. The girls *did* look valiant and brave, pretty nifty.

When the Workers' Mao Zedong Thought Propaganda Teams entered the universities in 1969, the working class were the masters of all. They actually screwed up everything. To tell the truth, though the PLA representatives were stern, they did pay attention to policy guidelines. Sending workers to run the schools was really the biggest mistake Mao made. Who in hell did they think they were? As far as they were concerned they were now top dog and didn't fear heaven or hell. As I told you, by then we Red Guards had lost all our standing. One worker said, "We, the working class, come to occupy the schools. Chairman Mao sends us!" They all came carrying plastic mangos, as Mao had once given mangos to a worker propaganda team. When the workers would lecture us they'd unbutton their shirts and prop their feet up on the tables. It's unbelievable now. There were a few old workers who had genuinely suffered a lot before Liberation. But they were just used as pawns by the young workers to gain respect and control the school. The old workers were sent to give us lectures about their past sufferings, but the real motive of the propaganda teams was to further persecute intellectuals. The workers were also on bad terms with the soldiers, who now had to play second fiddle.

Once a workers' team chief got the bright idea of taking us to the countryside to reform our ideology. Both the PLA and workers' propaganda teams marched right behind us. At the blow of a whistle we'd all plunge headlong to work in the paddy fields. Many of the girls were having their periods but didn't dare complain. Their legs got all puffy and filled up with fluid.

We also had "Morning Report for Instruction" and "Evening Report." Early in the morning, too exhausted to move from the day before, we had to stand in front of Mao's portrait and chant, "I intend to do this task today, Chairman Mao. I'm going to do it according to the quotation of yours that says. . . ." Going back in the evening, no matter how tired we were, we still didn't dare miss the ceremony. This time we reported, "Chairman Mao, today I did this and made such and such a mistake. . . ." Another thing the workers said we should do was to create a "Red Sea—a vast red expanse of Mao Zedong thought." So everything that didn't move, or at least stayed still long enough, got painted red. As Chairman Mao was our sun and we were his sunflowers, turning always toward him, we also spent lots of time painting sunflowers or making sunflower models.

At night there were mobilization drills. The moment you fell asleep, you'd be woken up to practice rapid march. No lights allowed. We'd have to put all our stuff in backpacks and march at least 15 km. I was really getting annoyed. They were torturing us on purpose. The second time it happened I refused to get up. I told the worker, "Don't you see how the girls are suffering?" I said it out of a sense of justice. "The hell with you," I said. "Do whatever you want to me." The worker got very mad and broke off the wooden handle of a sickle. "Bloody hell!" he yelled. "You're more revisionist than revisionists!" I yelled back, "Don't give me that crap. When my father was laboring as a worker, you weren't even born!" The military team member was understanding and reasonable. He pushed me aside, pretending to threaten me. "Go back and write a self-criticism," he told me. "Hand it in tomorrow morning. You'll be in big trouble if you don't." I refused. "You son of a bitch!" he cursed and struck me on the shoulder. He was on my side, I knew. If not for him, I would have been singled out for the crime of being "anti–working class." I was dashed. I was worthless. Me! A Red Guard!

Just before my graduation in the spring of 1970 rumors were spreading around the school that my father was a spy. They were probably started by those damned workers. A worker who was after my girlfriend took advantage of the situation. He kept going to see her and warn her what a bad influence I was. Finally he succeeded in splitting us up. I went to see my girlfriend and she cried for two hours but it was obviously over. Later I heard that she'd fallen in love with that guy. This is really personal. I never told anyone before. But you can see that everything that meant something to me was affected by the Cultural Revolution.

Our postgraduate job assignments were set by the workers' team. The rule was that "lovers go together to the farthest places; those with physical disabilities go to the nearest; and single people go to places in between." I belonged to the third category. When the final assignments were announced, I felt as though it was a prison sentence. The place you were sent to was where your fate lay. We were following Mao's directive that all graduates go to the countryside.

I believe that I'm a man of strong character. So much had happened to me and yet I managed to stay sane. When I left the school and my girlfriend behind, I naturally shed a few tears. All I carried away were some cartons of books. That's all I possessed. My teachers sent me off. I said to them, "I'm going to receive education from the poor and lower middle-class peasants. I will perform well and try to join the Party before I come back to visit you." I was always like that, full of enthusiasm.

But during the following years in the countryside and later, when I was teaching in a commune middle school, I just couldn't stay out of trouble no matter what I tried to do. I almost died in the Tangshan earthquake of 1976. The school buildings all collapsed. I'd been secretly reading the classic novel *Strange Stories From a Chinese Studio,* you know, all about ghosts, devils, immortals, and so on. When the calamity happened I felt a strange sense of relief. As though even gods and ghosts avoided me. Nothing seemed to matter anymore. I'd gotten into so much trouble for my efforts, failed to join the Party and felt like I was good for nothing. I just didn't care, the hell with everything. I purposely started to make trouble whenever I got the chance. Strangely enough, people were intimidated by me. But I still felt empty inside. What was I after, what did I really want? I didn't know. Life became meaningless.

After the fall of the Gang of Four, it suddenly dawned on me that I'd been cheated—all those years of being deceived. Yet even before I could make any sense of this new revelation, the "check-ups"[32] started and I was being checked. This campaign was supposedly for the stabilization of the country, but it turned out to be just another replay of one faction against another. People outside the Red Guards who had beaten and tortured others generally got left alone. As for us Red Guards, now in our thirties, we were the targets of check-ups. We were accused of five "crimes" and they were all fabricated, of course. When will these wrongs ever get righted? I feel very depressed these days. I often wonder, the world is so big, why do we have to be at each other's throats all the time? Don't people ever get fed up with it?

I'm a person who's full of energy but I've never really done anything for our country and I do want to find a way. I didn't get a real education; my degree is only so much paper. I've made a five-year plan to improve myself. I'm determined to study rhetoric and do something in that field. I've read as widely as I can and even got a few articles in linguistics published. I really am not after fame or fortune, I just want to find my place in this society, my identity. This country has trained me, but who am I? What have I really accomplished?

As I said, I have no regrets about my part in the Cultural Revolution. To thoroughly repudiate the movement politically is valid. I have no disagreement. But as a mass movement one cannot simply negate it, one cannot draw a simple political line. How to understand it? Well, let me give you a few of my own thoughts. I think the Central Committee is in a bind because China has never really escaped feudalism—by this I mean specifically the mentality of the people. One thing I clearly learned in my countryside experience was that the old system of connections still dominates everything. It's not what you do but rather who you know or who you're related to. It's like a giant web. Once you get caught up in it, you will never be able to disentangle yourself. That's why it's so hard to carry out reforms. For the sake of stability, the Central Committee totally repudiated the Cultural Revolution, and this was necessary. In politics there's no room for human feeling or honesty. It's like when you move into an old house: No matter how hard you try to clean up, there are always things that remind you of previous tenants. So you have to throw out good things as well as bad. But I feel that the Red Guards should not be repudiated. They should be analyzed from a historical perspective.

I'm sure future generations will vindicate us but it's too soon

99

to make a judgment on us now. So many plays, movies, and stories today portray the Red Guards as no better than the KMT or Nazi brownshirts. It's not fair. Maybe you can excuse some writers who are too young to have had any personal experience of the Cultural Revolution, but certainly not those who had. They're just irresponsible hacks. Hell, we were human too! Some movies show us attacking parents and leaving their children sprawled about, crying helplessly. Bullshit! We loved children too! Yes, the Red Guards movement was a catastrophe. But don't compare it with the Nazi brownshirts: The Red Guards were a spontaneous movement while the brownshirts were tools of the regime. They were totally different! I can't say I don't feel remorseful about my Red Guard past. But I'm not apologetic. There are things you can feel sorry for and things you cannot. Especially when you get to be my age.

There's another thing you've got to understand. All our lives we were brought up to believe that the Party was always right and of course, Chairman Mao was the Party. Our generation is still dedicated and patriotic in our goal to reform China. We're the most reliable age group in China, not like the old people who oppose anything new or the young who chase every rainbow. The most important thing comrade Mao Zedong gave me is class affinity. No matter what happens I will never become a degenerate or a criminal, not even in times of strife. However, there's something this kind of education gave me that I'll always hate. I was conditioned to blindly follow the leadership and never to think for myself. Mao was like old Lord Ye who professed to love dragons but surely didn't want one to visit. Mao told us to put down slavery and dogmatism, but look what happened when we took him literally.

I reckon I still have another thirty years or so of work left in me. All I want is to carry out whatever our country asks of me as well as I can. It's the only way I can feel whole again. That's all I have to say.

⚑

"The worst tragedy is to give loyalty and receive deception."—F. J.

FOOTNOTES

1. "Model students" of the 1960s who volunteered to forego cushy positions in the big cities to endure the hardships of life in the countryside.

2. Part of an autobiographical series of novelettes written by Zhang Xianliang describing the sufferings of those labeled Rightists and sentenced to prison camps and state farms after their release. Zhang Yonglin, the main protagonist, is a pseudonym for the author.

3. Before the Cultural Revolution, Mao had stated that people were divided into different classes on the basis of their family background, financial status, and political viewpoint, and that class struggle was going on all the time, everywhere. This theory was quoted with particular frequency during the Cultural Revolution.

4. It is a Chinese custom, especially in the countryside, to curse in public without naming names—but everyone generally knows who is being cursed.

5. A young soldier of the 1960s who died in service exemplifying the ideals to be followed by the new generation.

6. An opera about the sufferings of poor peasants before Liberation in 1949. It was later turned into a "model revolutionary ballet" by

order of Jiang Qing, who was Chairman Mao's wife and part of the Gang of Four.

7. A poor village in Shanxi Province. With tremendous effort farmers there terraced the barren hillsides to make them productive. Dazhai Brigade was held up as a model for the whole country during the Cultural Revolution.

8. A derogatory term applied to those who focused on academic studies to the exclusion of ideology.

9. Published in *People's Daily,* June 1, 1966, calling upon people to actively rid society of "bad elements."

10. Written by Deng Tuo (1912–1966), historian, poet, and essayist. He was the Party Secretary of Beijing in charge of cultural and educational work. Because of his series of essays, *"The Chats,"* he was labeled a counterrevolutionary during the Cultural Revolution and the study of his works was considered to be anti-Party and antisocialist.

11. A famous historian and professor at Beijing University who died under persecution during the Cultural Revolution for his supposedly anti-Party views.

12. Norman Bethune, Canadian surgeon and dedicated Communist, revered by the Chinese Communists as a revolutionary hero. He came to Yanan in 1938 and later founded the International Peace Hospital. He died in 1939 of blood poisoning contracted from a surgical accident.

13. A document properly titled "Decisions Concerning the Great Proletarian Cultural Revolution" promulgated by the Central Committee of the Chinese Communist Party. It spelled out the guidelines to be followed in the Cultural Revolution.

14. Lu Xun, pseudonym of Chou Shujen (1881–1936), is often considered the founder of modern Chinese literature and a key figure in the literary struggle to overthrow China's feudal social system.

15. Member of the ruling Politburo. He was persecuted for his efforts to defend President Liu Shaoqi and Deng Xiaoping (then general secretary of the Communist Party). Tao died in prison.

16. Xinhuamen is a gate to the west of Tiananmen.

17. The rostrum is located above the entrance to the Forbidden City. It is approached via the Jinshuiqiao moat bridge from Changan Avenue.

18. Lin Biao was killed in a plane crash in September 1971 while fleeing to the Soviet Union. The official announcement in 1972 stated that Lin had led an assassination attempt and coup against Mao.

19. Mao Dun (1896–1986), real name Shen Yanbing, was one of the most revered twentieth-century Chinese writers. Like Lu Xun, he was awakened early to the need to transform Chinese society and in his own words sought painstakingly for "a new method of expression which better fits the temper of the times."

20. Du Pengcheng was a military writer known best for his biography of Marshal Peng Dehuai, who was a critic of Mao's Great Leap Forward. Du was persecuted for daring to choose such a subject.

21. Tian Han (1898–1968), playwright, poet, author of China's national anthem, and a pioneer in Chinese modern drama. He died under persecution in the Cultural Revolution.

22. The headquarters of the Chinese Communists from 1936 to 1947. The Long March from Jiangxi ended in 1935 when the Red Army reached the northern Shaanxi town of Wuqi. They then moved their base to Yanan.

23. Appellation of the People's Liberation Army.

24. Elementary school Red Guards.

25. First "dictatorship of the proletariat," established by the French working class in 1871.

26. Russian counterintelligence agency (1917–1934).

27. During October 1933 Chiang Kai-shek mobilized one million troops in a massive attack against the Red Army bases in the Jiangxi and Fujian border areas. Because some unwise elements in the Communist Party hierarchy advocated meeting Chiang's troops in pitched battles, Mao's guerrilla warfare tactics were not used. By October 1934 the Red Army had suffered enormous losses and was pushed back to

their original base at Jinggangshan in the western mountains of Jiangxi. From here began the Long March north to Shaanxi.

28. Ordinary workers authorized by a directive from Mao to take administrative control of universities, research institutes, and government organs.

29. A counterrevolutionary; someone in power who followed "the capitalist road."

30. Anti-Party, Antisocialism, Anti–Mao Zedong thought.

31. Kuomintang terrorism.

32. A campaign initiated in 1977 to single out suspected followers of the Gang of Four at all levels of society (different from the "checkups" begun in 1967).

T H E
3 , 6 5 0   D A Y S
O F   A
C O U P L E

T I M E : *1966* ♙ A G E S : *Husband 26 / Wife 20*
O C C U P A T I O N : *Workers at a machine factory in T city*

HUSBAND: I hate to recall it. We always try to avoid the subject. Just mentioning it brings us nights on end with no sleep. And what's the use of dwelling on it? Now we're called on to look forward into the future, aren't we? Blame everything on the Gang of Four. Bury the horrors of the past. Too many people suffered and nobody wants to talk about it. But I figure our sufferings can't just be written off, right? I'll tell you about it if you'll get it into print so that it's on record and future generations can read about it.

I was jailed for ten years for nothing, no reason at all. My wife waited for me all that time and went through hell, a lot worse than me. What the hell did my punishment have to do with her?

It didn't matter that I had to suffer. I'm a man. But it was a lot harder on her. You imagine. She had only just turned twenty then. Good-looking, too. I've got an old photo of her. Have a look. She had to support her old paralyzed father and a newborn baby. She was treated as the dependent of a counterrevolutionary and her father was labeled a capitalist. Our apartment was occupied by neighborhood activists and she was forced to live in a small rundown room, and that collapsed during the earthquake. It wasn't easy for her to survive those ten years waiting for me. The divorce rate was over 90 percent for us prisoners. Many prisoners killed themselves or other people or went crazy because their wives left them. Each time she came to visit me in prison, the other inmates were pretty jealous. At first I didn't dare to say she was my wife. I was afraid she still might divorce me and I'd be too embarrassed.

Back then, of course, she didn't know the Gang of Four would be kicked out someday and I'd be rehabilitated. She was simply waiting for a counterrevolutionary. Even if I was released she'd still be looked down on. Nothing for her but political pressures all the time and always the money problems. She was so young and pretty that she could have found a way out. That's why I feel very proud of her. She has the strong character of a real Chinese woman. I feel this way and I'll say so no matter who I'm talking to.

Nothing special about me. A lot of people suffered more than I did. Many were jailed just for making some casual remark. Lots of the inmates were there as "active counterrevolutionaries." One cellmate of mine was once the head of his village peasant association. One day he came down from his mountain village to buy or, as we used to say, "to invite" some Chairman Mao plaster statues. An honorable job that was only for people with the right family backgrounds. To carry them more easily on the way back, he tied the statues by their necks and strung them over his shoulders, two in front and two in back. Well, you can imagine what that looked like to the crazies we had running around. They pounced on him before he got very far. He was arrested right there and got sentenced to five years as an active counterrevolutionary. How stupid can people get? Another young guy was jailed because of some bird's-eye view snapshots he took on top of a department store at night for his own collection. He was charged with spying. It was that guy who helped me to pass out a handkerchief to my wife. We still have it.

WIFE: Yes. The handkerchief was used by my husband to wrap his bleeding head the day he was arrested. They'd beaten him up with pointed steel bars. The handkerchief was soaked with blood. I've brought it with me. See the holes? They really were cold-blooded people. How could they be so cruel?

HUSBAND: Some other things they did to me were a lot worse. Sometimes it's hard to explain. The Public Security people weren't supposed to abuse us but I saw them torturing prisoners. A fine bunch. They weren't satisfied with handcuffs. They tied people up with heavy steel wires tightened with pliers. Some people's wrists got infected from that and turned white, with maggots living in them. Eh! Too much of that. Let's change the subject.

I said I'd focus on my wife. She suffered more and was a lot more special than me. Lots of so-called counterrevolutionaries, but very few wives like her. I suffered pretty badly, but I still got back with my wife and kid. Some people came out of prison with the wife divorced, children taken away, houses occupied, and the ex-wife now living with the person next door. How would you feel then?

OK. Let's start from the beginning. I'm from a working-class background. I had been a fitter and was in charge of the workshop production unit before the Cultural Revolution. I'm a straightforward person, never brownnosed the cadres. I often lodged complaints for my fellow workers even if the cadres didn't like it. That's why they tried to find fault with me right from the start of the Cultural Revolution. They said I wasn't close to the Party.

I'm sure they'd planned to persecute me. The excuse was something I'd said. In fact, it was just a joke. When I was drinking with some guys I worked closely with, I made a wise-crack about how the first Ming emperor suddenly killed all his loyal followers when he got himself on the throne. That got reported to the factory leaders as a slight on Chairman Mao. You couldn't trust anybody in those days. I didn't know until the next night, March second, 1968, that I'd been reported, and suddenly I found myself being denounced in a mass meeting as a counterrevolutionary. Instantly big-character posters went up all over the place. The shit really hit the fan! I was ferreted out! According to the posters, my family background had changed to a capitalist one instead of worker. Therefore I was planning a "class revenge." I don't know who wrote that stuff, but every-one jumped on the bandwagon. No way I could argue. At first it was only denunciation, but then the military representative shouted the slogan "Verbal struggle, no violence!" It was a prearranged signal. A bunch of bastards jumped me and began beating me really badly. They used angle irons and all kinds of things that were lying around. I couldn't tell who was attacking me; all I knew was to cover my head with my handkerchief and hands. I didn't bleed a lot; there was just a hell of a lot of sharp pain. I was almost killed. They all came down on my head, that's why the holes in the handkerchief. I'm still half deaf in one ear from that beating and I hear a ringing sound all the time. I passed out from their kicks and punches. They tied me up with steel wire and sent me to the police.

WIFE: I was there that day at the meeting. We worked in the same factory. The meeting was supposed to elect the factory revolutionary committee. When they started beating my husband, I didn't dare look. I was terrified and desperately wanted to be anywhere else. But the moment I got outside, the woman director of the revolutionary committee blocked my way and wouldn't let me go. That shows they had it all planned. Later, when I finally got home, a neighbor told me my husband had been brought home for a few minutes by the factory people. "Did he have a traffic accident?" she asked me. Inside the room I saw blood, blood everywhere.

If he hadn't been taken then, I guess he would have suffered a lot worse later on during the "cleanup" campaign and other movements. He'd have been at least crippled if not killed. That kind of people wouldn't have let him off so easily.

HUSBAND: The charges against me weren't straightened out till 1970. I was not a capitalist descendant and not bad enough to be an active counterrevolutionary. But the military representative and the revolutionary committee refused to admit their mistakes. They refused to rehabilitate me, supposedly to safeguard their revolutionary standing. That military bastard hadn't got what he wanted yet. He was after my wife. As for the prison, they just treated us like goods in a warehouse. One warden told me, "It doesn't make any difference to me where you are. I'll release you when I get a bill of lading." That's what he really said. So I stayed locked up for those ten long years. When I was released, my sister said, "You were tortured half to death just for the two pieces of paper of your sentence." I have the two papers with me. Look! They were so carelessly scribbled, not even as formal as a bill of lading. Another warden once said to us, "Our job is to imprison and release people. You guys stop making trouble for us. If you're fed up with living, then go kill yourselves. I don't even have to write a report of negligence in my work if you do. I don't give a shit who is alive and who's dead."

WIFE: My husband was first locked up in the detention office of the Public Security Bureau. I was terrified that he might be given a really bad sentence and sent to a faraway place because of his hot temper and straightforwardness. If he was jailed in the city, at least I'd be allowed to see him once a month or so. Just to see each other would be a comfort. I was so scared he might be sent to Qinghai or Tibet or places like that. That would have killed me.

I thought the prisoners then looked like stage actors. In the public sentencings there were always dozens of them getting sentenced at once. They were carried in trucks on display from one place to another, from stadiums to theaters, then to schools and factories. They were like actors rushing to give a performance and the play was always the same: People gathered, prisoners were escorted to the front, their crimes were listed, and finally came the sentence. Public sentencing was to deter other people, especially people like me, timid and honest.

HUSBAND: In jail my job for quite a while was to fix handcuffs, big baskets of them. They were always in demand. Many, many people were arrested, sometimes hundreds at once. Words could kill. One word out of place and you were in jail. Too many people there were like me. My wife didn't want me to make trouble. I understood. I already felt guilty about her. I got to know some other inmates very well and we helped each other. We had a world of our own. None of us had criminal records; we'd all committed the same kind of "crime." We became good friends. Even now we often visit with each other.

WIFE: We got married on the Lunar New Year's Day of 1968. My husband was taken away on March second. We'd only had sixty days together. I survived the next ten years by recalling our happy times during the honeymoon, my trust in him, and counting the 3,650 days one by one.

Only twenty, just out of school and working for the first time, my husband turning overnight into an active counterrevolutionary—it was almost too much for me to take. The military representative and that woman director schemed together to get rid of my husband and force me into a divorce. They used every trick they could come up with. Even now I'm not sure how I resisted their attempts. Maybe I'm tougher than I look.

After my husband was arrested, my apartment was ransacked six times. Our quilts, blankets, clothes, and wedding presents were all taken away. Finally only a bare bed was left. The factory put up a display of all the things ransacked. I was too numb to care anymore and let them loot whatever they wanted. What could I do about it anyway? I couldn't hate the looters because they were all from the right family backgrounds and were defending the red revolutionary dictatorship of the people. Let them risk their lives and show off their revolutionary spirit.

One thing that made me feel very fortunate was that I kept our most valuable gift for my husband, our son Xiao Dong. As you know, Dong means "winter" since he was born in the winter. I could cut hair and make clothes, and I had to make clothes for my son to save money. My fellow workers asked me to help them too, but if I didn't do it right they'd insult me. And if I did too good a job, I'd be criticized for going in for fancy styles. I had to use my husband's lunchbox with his name still on it and got criticized for not making a clean break with him. Lots of that kind of thing. In those days, no matter what you did, someone would pick on you.

When Xiao Dong was born, I didn't even have a quilt. We just slept on the bare bed. I put my husband's letters under my pillow so I could feel he was closer to me and he might possibly feel the happiness of having a son. I knew if I believed it strongly enough, he would.

I only had fifty-six days of maternity leave but on the fifty-third day my baby got pneumonia and was very sick. It was winter. My room was freezing. I was only twenty that year and knew very little about how to look after babies. That night my son was very quiet and I thought he was getting better. But the next morning I saw his face turning blue. I had no money to go see a doctor. My neighbors were too frightened to have anything to do with me so I couldn't borrow from them. My child was dying. As a last resort I called my mother-in-law and asked her to come. That day happened to be when the latest directive from Mao was released and the whole city stopped working for a parade and celebration. It was always like that in those days. People packed the streets. No buses. Everything stopped. It took my mother-in-law several hours to walk all the way to my place. We sent my son to the city's children's hospital and he was finally saved.

HUSBAND: When I got her letter and learned she was going to have a baby the next month and couldn't come to see me, I had very mixed feelings. I wasn't prepared for the sudden news. I was going to be a father. But what had I brought to my wife and our child-to-be? My child would be labeled the bastard of a counterrevolutionary from the moment he came into the world. It was all my fault. I hated myself. I had failed them both.

I had no idea our home had been looted and that nearly all our relatives had refused to keep in touch with my wife. She was supporting herself, her paralyzed father, our child—all on seventeen yuan a month as a factory apprentice. A dog's wage! Yet she still managed to buy cigarettes and other things for me. You try to imagine how it was.

WIFE: The child was our lifeblood. When he was asleep I'd study every feature; his smile and the way he slept were so much like his father. With tears in my eyes I'd spend the nights thinking about the too few days we'd had together. My husband told me in his letters that he always dreamed of Xiao Dong at night. Although our son only knew his father from the prison visits, a deep bond was formed from the beginning. Whenever we had some good food, Xiao Dong would always want to share it with his father. One year during the National Day fireworks celebration he asked Grandma if Dad could see them too. He was overjoyed when she told the boy he could.

My husband often pestered me to get photos of Xiao Dong taken so he could see his son growing every day. He hid the photos between the pages of Mao's "Little Red Book" to look at secretly. No matter how tight things were, I'd always find a bit of extra money for those photos.

HUSBAND: I saw the movie *The Sparkling Red Star* in prison. The boy in it was called Dong Zhi and of course he made me miss Xiao Dong very much. Another incident I still remember clearly was when I committed some sort of error and got punished for it. I complained in private to some other inmates, which added another crime to my name, "not admitting my own guilt." The punishment was to lose my visiting privileges. It just happened that that day Xiao Dong had come with his mother and he wasn't feeling very well. He had some apples with him that my wife usually couldn't afford to get him unless he was sick. He had insisted on bringing them for me. Well, they weren't allowed to see me but they left the apples behind. Just looking at them made me feel miserable. I had failed my family so terribly. The better they were to me, the worse I felt. It was their lasting love that got me through all those damn years. Each month we were only allowed fifteen minutes together. Sometimes you couldn't make out a single word because of the noise. I just tried to smile. I wanted to say a lot but didn't know how. My smile meant a lot. It was both an apology and also a way to show my determination to get an early release. It meant more than words.

I was so happy to see all the little changes in my son each time he came. I memorized all his words and gestures so I could recall them when I was alone. That was my greatest pleasure. Xiao Dong would often ask me when I'd come home and if I would take him to parks and places. What could I say? He was so loving to his "bad" father.

Once I was very sick and got sent to the hospital. Xiao Dong, my wife, and my mother came to see me. It was a very special meeting, the only time in the ten years that we could talk freely.

For the first time I held my son in my arms. He was so happy. When it was time to leave, he kept walking backward, smiling at me, and waving his little arms at me until he was out of sight. It . . . , it hurts me so to think of all those lost years. . . .

WIFE: Children nowadays are much better off. They have all sorts of toys and modern playthings. But Xiao Dong never had anything. We were dependents of a convicted class enemy and no one would have anything to do with us. I couldn't find anyone to look after Xiao Dong while my father and I were at work, and I didn't have the money for nursery school. I had to keep him locked up alone in the room. Once a neighborhood granny told me she saw Xiao Dong sucking the ice that had frozen to the mop. There was nothing to play with, nothing to do at all. Another time I came back from work and saw my father and Xiao Dong having fun lighting little candles—the closest thing to a toy for him. It broke my heart watching them. . . .

Each Spring Festival other families were enjoying themselves, but not us. Other kids, like his own cousins, would get new clothes to dress up in, but none of the family ever remembered to give him anything. I at least made him a pair of new shoes. He was so easy to please. I always tried to save a bit of Lunar New Year food for my husband. Xiao Dong would pick out the best of the few good things we had for the empty place we set. That was how we spent our New Year. It was torture.

One day a friend gave Xiao Dong a little bird. He wasn't sure about accepting it and asked me if the bird had a mommy and daddy. I said yes, of course. The next moment he was sobbing. "If we take away the bird," he cried, "he won't be able to see his daddy just like me." He opened his little hands and set the bird free. This is my child, so, so . . . I don't know how to say it.

My father was labeled a capitalist and forced to do hard labor even though he was half-paralyzed. Once they had him peeling leeks. The cleaver somehow got buried in the piles of leeks. He was accused of planning a class revenge murder with the missing cleaver. He just fell apart, broke down, and cried. Thank God I finally found the cleaver for him. Father saved every bit of what little money he got and wrapped each coin in paper. We could only manage 20 fen of meat each month, less than 200 grams back then. We even sold the copper knobs off our furniture to buy some decent flour for Xiao Dong.

I wasn't afraid of hardship; all I asked for was a quiet and peaceful life. But even this was too much to hope for.

The woman director worked hand in glove with the military representative. They asked me to get a divorce. First they tried to get me on their side. I had no idea that they had schemes about me. They went to a lot of trouble and located my mother who I hadn't even known. She turned out to be a poor farmer. She had sold me to my childless capitalist adoptive father. He was very nice to me and always treated me like his own daughter. Now they told me that I was the child of peasants and they would help me out. They wanted me to make a total break with my husband and adoptive father. The woman director said, "If you divorce him, we'll give you a new place to live and all your things back. You can even join the Party and I'll find a new husband for you. You can count on me." That military guy was from the countryside. He followed me everywhere. He would talk to me for a whole day at a time. I wasn't even left alone to work in the workshop. Whenever there was a meeting, he'd drag me there. He'd call for me anywhere, even in front of a crowd. Keeping face didn't matter at all to him. The director told me that the apartment was ready and they were just waiting for my revolutionary action. They claimed the Party was concerned and responsible for me. They brought in my mother and a brother from the countryside and told her to give a lecture to the whole factory about how badly she had suffered before Liberation. A bunch of workers were organized too as a committee to persuade me. They told me that the only way I could prove I had returned to the ranks of the masses was by divorcing. That soldier would say to me, "You're our working-class sister. How can I not want to look after you?" He said he wasn't good with words. He was constantly thinking of me, so he said, even having sleepless nights over me and lots of other rubbish like that. It was really ridiculous.

My mother and brother asked me to agree to the divorce as a stopgap. They were afraid I'd suffer too much otherwise. My mother finally ran away back to the countryside. She couldn't stand to see me suffer anymore. She hated that director.

Meanwhile, the director said she'd take care of my marriage. The soldier and director were just using me to help each other. If he married a city girl, he wouldn't have to go back to the countryside after demobilization; she was building up her position for promotion. Later on both of them got themselves named to the "three-in-one" committee controlling the factory.

They pressed me very hard for a long time. I'd be kept late at the factory and my father would always be waiting, worried something had happened to me. Once he broke down and said he wanted to go to Beijing to lodge complaints. It was too much for me. I wrote to my husband suggesting we get divorced so they would leave me alone. It might make it easier for me to go back to him later. He replied at once. I have the letter here:

April 28, 1971

Chairman Mao tells us:

THINGS ARE CONSTANTLY CHANGING. TO ADAPT ONE'S MIND TO THE NEW CIRCUMSTANCES, ONE MUST STUDY CONTINUOUSLY.

Dear (wife's name),

How are you? I've been formally informed of your decision to cut off relations with me. It's the right choice and I understand your reasons. I resolutely support you.

I won't obstruct you in any way in the divorce. The initiative is in your hands anyway. I'm a prisoner. My only wish is to keep the child. To me he is the single hope and promise left in my life. I have to consider the future. I have no intention of getting a stepmother for him and will never do so. I'm not a flighty person. You should know that. You can probably imagine what will become of me in ten years.

If you want another child, you can still have one. It's different for me. Please honor my request and, in short, I'll look upon the divorce question with the right attitude.

Wishing you success on your chosen path,

Your husband ———

WIFE: I was very sad when I read his reply. Though we loved each other, our time together had been too short and the separation was too long. There was no chance to develop our feelings. But to marry someone else . . . ? I went to the local judicial office. There, to my surprise, I was told that my factory had already sent people to arrange a divorce for me. I was shocked. They were way ahead of me. Luckily even back then there were some decent people around. The judicial worker told me a divorce had to be settled by the two parties concerned. A third party couldn't arrange it. He added, "If you leave him, he'll be much worse off in prison. Can't you understand that?" I felt like I'd been saved at the last minute. I'd found legal protection. I wouldn't start a divorce.

The factory director was furious. "You've won!" she screamed. "You've beaten us all!" I was sent to dig air raid shelters as punishment. But I was tough. I worked hard. The next torment was big-character posters going up in the factory denouncing me as my adoptive father's concubine. At that time people would write whatever insults they could think of. Sometimes in despair I considered suicide. But the thought of my husband and son kept me going. As long as my son and I stayed alive, my husband would have something to hope for. For better or worse, I'd make it through.

The hardest time was during the '76 earthquake. Our room

collapsed. Nobody took care of us. There was no one to help me gather the bricks for a temporary shelter. We just hung a piece of tarpaulin over some barbed wire and packed mud on the sides. It washed off whenever it rained. No electricity either. We had to make do with a kerosene lamp. At night the winds were very strong. The three of us had to huddle together to sleep. It was like that for a couple of years.

HUSBAND: In my first few years in prison our letters had to be exactly correct to get by the chief warden. We didn't dare try to speak our minds. Later on, things improved a little, but you have a look at some of these letters I've kept and you'll see what I mean:

August 7, 1968

WISHING CHAIRMAN MAO LONGEVITY!
LONG LIVE CHAIRMAN MAO!
Dear Father and Mother,
    I hope you are well.
    As I didn't pay attention to the revered Chairman Mao's teachings and didn't act according to his directives, I have committed serious crimes and made very bad errors. The revolutionary masses, in order to rescue me, have sent me to the Public Security Bureau for reeducation. Now I'm studying and going through ideological reform in the Mao Zedong Thought Study Course under the leadership of the People's Liberation Army. Do not worry. I'm determined to turn over a new leaf. . . .

March 8, 1975

Chairman Mao teaches us:
THE CHANGE IN ONE'S OUTLOOK
IS A FUNDAMENTAL CHANGE.

Dear (wife's name),

Your two letters this month have reached me. I understand that you're worried I haven't reformed myself conscientiously enough. I feel very contrite toward you and our son. I have realized the seriousness of my mistakes in humble gratitude to the reeducation given me by the chief warden. I'm determined to deepen my understanding of my guilt through studying the theory of proletarian dictatorship and to achieve a clear picture of the damage I have done to the Party and the masses. I will give up all my misconceptions and reform myself in a practical way. . . .

[HUSBAND: Hah! By "misconceptions" here, I meant my repeated complaints to the higher authorities. Their replies usually went something like this: "There are some mistakes in the wording of your sentence. We can drop 'class revenge' and your family background can be reclassified as 'working class.' But of course these matters will have to wait for the moment as we are busy defending the fruits of victory of the Great Proletarian Cultural Revolution."

"Fruits of victory" my foot! What it really boiled down to was that they were in cahoots with the PLA propaganda team. They would never admit the way they had treated me was wrong. That's why they refused to rehabilitate me.]

. . . Please do not worry. I won't do anything to hurt you in the future. Each time I see your tearstains on the envelope and the letter brings your image to me.

I did make up my mind to reform myself, but my misconceptions were too strong. I was often painfully disappointed. . . .

I wrongly refused to see the seriousness of my crimes. I wouldn't open my heart and soul to our leaders, but instead confided my true feelings secretly to some individuals. I even started to resent the chief warden in spite of his patient attention. I failed our Party, the chief warden, you, and our son. From now on I will always heed the chief warden's teachings. I have realized that the Party is my true family. They will guide me on the ideologically correct path. For as Chairman Mao has said, "There will always be a bright future for those who have seen the error of their ways."

After reading your letters, the chief warden told me I should think about my family. He has racked his brains to educate me so that I can be reunited with you sooner.

One of my major problems is my lack of a clear understanding of my crimes. Under the guidance of the chief, I will study official documents and papers including Yao Wenyuan's[1] "On the Social Basis of Lin Biao's Anti-Party Clique" to discover the social root causes of my guilt. My outlook on life is still bourgeois and my ideological level is still low. Therefore I hope you will give me lots of help in the future. . . .

[HUSBAND: You see what I mean about writing for the chief warden? I was asked to trace the class roots of my crimes. I'm a worker, how in hell can I find a bourgeois root? I had to admit to crimes I didn't do and criticize myself. With what little education I have, how can I come up with correct political theory answers? But then if you didn't tell the chief what he wanted to hear, you'd lose visiting privileges. I couldn't handle that. Even so, if you read carefully, some real thoughts still come through the double-talk.]

October 9, 1974

Dear (wife's name),

The 10th Party Congress has just concluded. We have been holding heated discussions and study sessions of the resolutions. This has reinforced our resolve to reform ourselves. Even I have been full of enthusiasm lately. My confidence in the Party's policy has never been stronger. Do not worry about me. I'm fine and in good shape, though I'm getting a bit old. I weigh sixty-eight kilos now. Our food is very good and I have a healthy appetite. I feel better mentally and have fewer misconceptions.

How are you lately? Your health? Work? I'm very much concerned about your life. I haven't heard from you for a couple of months and have no idea what's going on. What is it like at home? Who else can tell me if not you? I figure the time is drawing near when they'll release me....

I had to say good things about my health or my family would worry too much. Actually we had stinking grub like steamed bread made of cornstarch, and sorghum, and stale vegetables. Once a year on New Year's Eve we'd get a treat of dumplings. I remember one National Day when we actually got something special—a small piece of stewed pork each. It should have been a real treat since I hadn't had meat for so long, but somehow the sight of it made me sick and I threw up. I was too dumb to know I'd been suffering from jaundice.

WIFE: When he was released in 1978 I felt like I was in a trance. I had been dreaming of him coming home for so long that I could hardly believe it was really happening. We were still stuck in a temporary shack, but now I felt warm and comforted. We were finally a whole family.

The first night he was back we hardly spoke, just sat there staring at each other. I felt as if I was ten years younger again. I couldn't ask him about prison, we'd been through too much already. Our nerves were too weak. Enough pain already. I watched him finally fall asleep and thought of 3,650 nights I had spent with the moon and stars. I couldn't hold back my tears....

I thought that at last I'd have somebody to rely on, but he was a lot weaker than me. He couldn't handle any problems. He sat there in bed every day, not moving, with a heavy quilt wrapped around him. He didn't talk to me, only gave me blank stares.

My husband used to talk and joke a lot. Prison had totally changed him. Our shack had a tiny window, but he insisted on covering half of it with newspaper. He felt better in the gloom. He was afraid of light, noise, or any sudden rustlings from outside. All bones, skinny as a straw. Ahh, a gust of wind could have blown him away.

When he was in jail we wrote each other quite a lot. Reading his letters was as close as I could come to talking to him. Even though he wrote them so they'd get through, they were still in his own hand. I wrote him a lot too. It's a pity all my letters were destroyed when he was released. They wouldn't allow him to take out a single piece of paper.

HUSBAND: Her letters were much better written than mine. She loves reading books, not like me. I wish I still had those letters. We never show mine to our son. Wouldn't do him any good and it's too painful to talk about anyway. Besides, knowing too much about my past might sow some seeds of revenge in him and give him some unhealthy ideas. That would ruin him. It's better that he makes some progress and follows our government's policies closely. So we seldom mention those days, just pretend nothing happened.

WIFE: It's impossible not to think about what happened. My husband has got back a lot of his old self in the past few years, though he still doesn't like to talk very much and prefers to be left alone. Today, when he talked so much to you, is more like he was before the Cultural Revolution. When he got out I felt like he was a stranger to me, not just in looks, but all over. Totally different. He was like an idiot. His mind had stopped working. Everything was wrong with him. Another person. . . .

Our son's grown up now. He's in high school. He's a strange boy, doesn't fit in with other kids, doesn't like to play with them. The neighborhood granny often mentions things about Xiao Dong's sad childhood. He never went through the naughty stage; he grew up early. He didn't like to join other children because he was afraid they'd ask him where his father worked and he stayed out of quarrels in case they'd use this sore point against him. Xiao Dong has very poor health because of the lousy diet we lived on. He was still bedwetting even at ten. He's so weak and fragile. Now that my husband has got the wages he was owed paid back, he often takes Xiao Dong out to buy good food. He wants to make up for those years.

HUSBAND: Yeah, when I was rehabilitated I was given back 4,000 yuan, the wages they owed me. Ten years in prison; 4,000 yuan. Shit! Four million wouldn't be enough for ten years of my life. Who the hell wants to sit in prison for ten years for no reason? When I got locked up I was a strong healthy young man. What was I like when I got out? An old useless wreck. Think about how much I went through! Nowadays some private traders can make a thousand yuan in one day. Does that mean my ten years are only worth four days of theirs?

I demanded to be allowed to return to the factory after my release, but the factory director answered, "If that guy wants to come back, break his legs first." They refused to accept me or even lend me money. No work, no money, and no decent place to live. I was full of hope at first when I was set free. I went to see the housing people straight off. The man on duty told me the guy in charge of rehabilitated prisoners was having a day off. I went back again and again, but he still gave me the same runaround. I found out later that he was the person in charge. Even now my housing still hasn't been settled. It's no use telling you this anyway. Rehabilitation will never mean anything for us nobodies. It just lets the leaders and famous people keep up the appearance of fairness. Don't you agree?

On top of it all, the bastards who persecuted me are still

doing fine, top dogs every one of them. I wasted ten years, ten goddamn long years! Even my present wage is three grades lower than theirs. I'll never catch up. Who wouldn't feel pissed off? I'm very angry. Sometimes I get it out by cursing to the four winds in the street. When they got down on me, there was no law to speak of. Now when the law is enforced, they all go scot-free. I'm telling you I've had it! It's time for me to get my revenge and let those bastards taste what it's like to suffer. While I was still in jail I began to think about it. Locking me up, trying to force my wife to divorce me, all the stuff they did to me! I thought about how I'd do it. No hurry, I'd be patient. As the saying goes, "For a real man ten years is not too long to wait for vengeance." I waited.

How? Well, I didn't fight with them. I wanted to torture them mentally. I remember those who beat me and persecuted me and plotted against me. When I got my wages back, I threw a banquet in the fancy Peace Restaurant. I sent an invitation to every one of them. I worded it very nicely: "I put all the blame on the Gang of Four. I'm looking ahead into the future. You persecuted me before but you were victims too. I'm not so narrow-minded. Let bygones be bygones. Since we can't avoid each other, let's act as though nothing has happened. We're still good friends." Guess what happened? None of those dog turds showed up. They knew better. I had nothing to fear and nothing to hide. If they had come, I really would have given them a piece of my mind.

Later on the factory Party Secretary often visited us, trying to pacify me. He was afraid I'd make trouble for him too. He promised to find me a house and said if I had any problems, I should come talk to him. He also made it clear that if I didn't make trouble for him, he wouldn't make trouble for me. I told him, "Don't you give me that crap. Fine. OK. You return my writing desk." I knew the desk taken away during the ransacking was being used by the factory manager. I didn't give a damn who was using it. I wanted to see them all embarrassed. No one warned us before we were ransacked. Also a table in the clinic was mine. They said they'd buy me new ones, but no, I said, I wanted my own. That's final. Put them in my backyard. They did and I smashed them all to pieces on the spot. And my quilts! I shredded them in their faces. I had to get it out and show them. My wife and baby had slept on a bare bed. Just seeing the quilts again drove me crazy. Some of the other things had been sold off; I couldn't do much about that.

Some of the people who had persecuted me the most were too scared to stay on in the factory. They got themselves transferred as soon as I returned. I ran into the former revolutionary committee director once at the entrance of the work unit she shifted to. I spat at her and shouted, "Your mother was a whore!" She pretended not to hear me, but guilt was written all over her. I wanted to make her lose as much face as I could for the wicked things she did.

There was also the coworker who reported me. I wouldn't let him off easily. I often went to visit him at home to make him suffer. As soon as I came around, the whole family'd get fidgety. I kept going there, watching TV, chatting with him. He was polite but he couldn't hide his nervousness. He knew I knew. Probably he was afraid I'd put poison in their teacups. One day I went there to borrow some tools. He showed me his toolbox and I picked out a scraper. Then I asked for a whetstone to hone it very, very sharp. He stood there watching me, blinking like mad, as if I were about to cut his throat with it. But he had nerve; he didn't break down then. After a few years, though, he changed. He got skinny and sickly. That's what I did to this guy.

A few of the others who beat me tried to avoid me too. They should. They ought to feel guilty, damn it, for what they did to me.

I should mention there were some coworkers who were decent to us. After I was arrested they often sneaked my wife some good vegetables for New Year and took care of her and the kid when they were sick. I will never forget them. Like people say, "A perilous path is a true test of the heart."

WIFE: Yes, they helped us survive. Everything had to be done secretly. Otherwise they would have gotten into trouble too. What hurt the worst was that most of our relatives faded into the woodwork as if we didn't exist. We were so badly off that our bad luck might have rubbed off on them. But after the fall of the Gang of Four, when our troubles were over and especially when the money was paid, they all popped up suddenly. One after another. I'm polite enough but I don't have any feelings for them. Well, maybe it's understandable. Who wanted trouble for themselves in those days? I don't really hate them.

There's something I want to tell you. Though we suffered so much, I don't blame anybody. What's the use? I only hope honest people like us will never suffer such bad luck ever again. We ordinary people don't have any power or connections. We have no way out once misfortune lands on us. We have to suffer. Now, I'm quite content. None of my family died or got maimed. We got united finally and have a nice son. That's enough for me. Anyway, that's how I feel.

"That which has not been destroyed by the ten-year holocaust will endure forever."—F. J.

FOOTNOTE

1. Yao Wenyuan, one of the Gang of Four, became a Politburo member during the Cultural Revolution and was responsible for Party propaganda and mass media.

T H E S E
T H I R T Y
Y E A R S
O F   M I N E

TIME: *1966* ❧ AGE: *50* ❧ SEX: *Male*
OCCUPATION: *Senior engineer in a civil engineering design institute in T city.*

I'm getting old and old people tend to be long-winded. Do you think you'll get bored? If not, I'll tell you about myself. Well, this life of mine! Where do I start? To talk about the Cultural Revolution, I'll have to say a few words about the ten years before and after. Altogether thirty years, the causes and the effects of those thirty years are closely connected.

I was officially labeled a Rightist at the age of forty, was sent back to my hometown at fifty, retired at sixty, returned to the city, and now I've reached seventy.

I left home and went to school when I was fourteen—started working six years later. I was working on railroad design before and after Liberation. In 1956 I was ranked as a senior intellectual, an associate professor. Have a government certificate to prove it too! I am expert in several specialties. In addition I've got practical experience such as in construction and management. I was in my prime, really the technological backbone of my institute. I'm not bragging here, but quite a number of the main railroads in the country were designed and constructed under my supervision and guidance. I was full of drive in those days and often got so excited about my work that I couldn't sleep at night.

Trouble first caught up with me during the Four Greats[1] movement of 1957. I was forty then. A Party branch secretary said to me, "You're a person who carries weight in this place. If you don't take the lead in expressing your views, the movement will never get off the ground here." There was something in what he said, I thought. So all right, I'll do it. I wrote up a big-character poster and trouble immediately followed.

I didn't actually have any complaints about the Party—at least nothing worth talking about. I also knew that I couldn't just fabricate something. However, I did find some of the workers and peasants turned cadres in the institute quite unpleasant. I was one of the founding members and knew the backgrounds of most of the people working there. Those cadres didn't have the foggiest idea about professional design work. So they got themselves put in charge of political affairs and personnel where they could lord it over other people. Once a personnel cadre wrote a letter of introduction for me in connection with some business matters, but it was full of mistakes. Well, I just listed such things in my poster.

That opened a can of worms. The Four Greats turned into the "Antirightist" campaign overnight. I was accused of "attacking the Party's personnel policy" and things like that. They said I had made anti-Party statements. One example was that I supposedly said, "The Luo-Zhang Clique[2] was very courageous," thus eulogizing the Rightists. How could I dare to say things like that? In fact I had once said to a colleague in private, "The people were very bold to oppose the Party like that." My colleague exposed me and twisted my words. Just for this, this trivial matter, I got the Rightist label.

There were five hundred intellectuals in the institute and eighty-eight of us became Rightists. That was about 17 percent. All of them were of course rehabilitated later. They were all wrongly judged. But I was puzzled: Even Chairman Mao said that only 1 to 3 percent of the intellectuals were Rightists. How did our institute manage to have so many?

Thank heaven my punishment was not the severest. After criticism and confessions, I was demoted from senior engineer to ordinary engineer and my salary cut from 146 yuan to 127.[3] Really first-class treatment for a Rightist. Still, once you were labeled, you had to bear a lot of political pressure. Anyway, I had nothing to complain about really and I just disciplined myself to work hard. I figured maybe in a couple of years the label would be taken off. My mistakes could only become less and less serious, not the other way around. Right?

However, things didn't work out the way one figured they would. As time went by, my problems got increasingly serious. At first when there was construction work, I'd be called on to be the team leader. Later I was only allowed to do design work. I didn't mind as long as I was able to use my skills and intelligence. But in 1959 a directive came from the top stating that Rightists should not engage in professional work: Only manual labor was permitted. So I was engaged in geological survey but all I did was dig holes. I worked like mad thinking that I would never be able to get rid of my Rightist label if I didn't really knock myself out. During the day I did physical labor and at night I was called on to help out with design. I managed to do it no matter how tired I was. Over a thousand kilometers of railroad near Zhangjiakou City was designed by me during two months of night work. It wasn't too bad really. Extra hours didn't bother me. At least I was still allowed to use my mind.

In 1963 the institute set up a farm mainly for growing vegetables. It was a time when food was in short supply. The farm was intended to make us self-sufficient and I was sent to work there. This time I was totally cut off from my profession. Most of the people sent there were Rightists, as well as some counter-revolutionaries and other "bad elements." In short, we were all "evil." The worst job was collecting night soil. To do it, you first drove a cart to the sewage pond in the residential area to collect the stuff and then hauled it back to the farm. I was the fittest and strongest, over six feet tall and a fearless cart driver. I volunteered to do the work. When the sewage was fermented it had a thick crust on top and we had to use big ladles to get at the liquid underneath. Often it would splash over our faces and clothes. I thought about it and improved the ladle design. I also made some steel pipes and outfitted the cart with them. It doubled the efficiency of the work. Well, the farm workers got to like me and the young people started calling me Chief.

About this time I heard that the government issued a directive about the delabeling of Rightists. We had a quota of three and one-half people for the whole institute. I didn't quite understand the half, but people told me that it was based on some ratio. Word got to me that I was on the list of those to be delabeled. I was beside myself with joy! I kept working hard and waiting hopefully, but nothing happened. Later we were told that during the Lushan Conference[4] the disgraced Peng Dehuai had spoken out in favor of moderation. The delabeling was canceled. Instead there would be a stronger class struggle campaign. Some posters appeared on the farm saying that the young workers were not steadfast enough in their revolutionary stance and were getting too close to the Rightists. Because of that no one dared to have anything to do with me again. I was really disappointed. I had thought that if I performed well, I would be able to get rid of my label, but it just became a heavier and heavier burden.

The next year all research institutes were called upon to "step out of the research facilities and go into society." The offices were deserted and locked up. Everyone was off to construction sites. Complete havoc. We Rightists went too. There were many tasks nobody could do, so they had to turn to me. For instance, a cross-section layout was needed. After everyone else had knocked off for the day, I was asked to come in at night. I had to work in secret right from the start as the directive had stated that Rightists weren't even allowed to touch the drafting board. I worked for over forty nights and finished a very accurate scale drawing. On the drawing, I wrote one line of neatly printed characters, each one measuring 2.5 mm in size. Meticulous, detailed work. Everyone praised my work. Later, it became famous throughout the institute.

Apart from physical labor and my nighttime drawing, I also helped out in the kitchen washing dishes, cleaning vegetables, sweeping floors, dumping burnt coal, all sorts of things. Every morning before the workers got up, we Rightists would carry buckets of water for washing up to their doors. We did all the menial tasks. The cook told us, "Life has been a lot easier for us since you people came."

A cadre told me that they were again considering delabeling me. He didn't sound like he was playing games with me but this time, before I even had time to get excited, the Cultural

Revolution started. I just knew then that there was no hope to remove my Rightist "hat."

When we got back to the institute, it was already in full swing. A revolutionary committee was set up and under it was a bunch of noisy louts who called themselves the Defending-Red-Power Death Squad. They were young and strong. Many of the senior intellectuals' living quarters had been ransacked. They themselves were being severely attacked. They were labeled "monsters" and sent off to the "cowshed." More than ten committed suicide by drowning themselves, jumping off buildings, cutting their throats, and so on. At first I wasn't singled out, partly I guess because I had been working hard to reform myself and partly because I kept a low profile. Also, according to Mao's directives, Rightists who kept their work and salary should stay in their work units to pursue their reform and would not be sent back to their hometowns. They should be treated differently from other "bad elements." Since I belonged in this category, I figured that if I just worked hard and kept my mouth shut, perhaps nothing would happen to me.

On the second of September, 1968, I was heating the big wood stove in the kitchen with another engineer. The stove had five openings. The weather was very hot and we were working shirtless. Suddenly several members of the Death Squad showed up yelling at us to take our things and follow them. Something was definitely wrong, but I didn't dare ask what. Just had to follow them.

As soon as we were led into the room they shoved us. "Now," they said, "you people admit your crime and ask Chairman Mao for forgiveness!" A Mao portrait was hanging on the wall. Aha! I thought. This ceremony just meant kowtowing. OK. I bowed three times. One of the louts immediately slapped me in the face. "Don't you even know how to do it?" I thought maybe I was short of the quota so I hurriedly added another two bows. That still wouldn't do. Then I was enlightened as to the fact that in bowing before Chairman Mao you had to do even numbers. We Rightists hadn't been privileged to take part in the mass rallies and demonstrations. How could we know the proper etiquette? So, for this horrendous slip, I got locked up in the "cowshed."

The same afternoon I was dragged to a struggle session with the words "Old Rightist" hung around my neck. There were another three counterrevolutionaries also being denounced. I thought they were the main targets; I just got a supporting role. But when the meeting was coming to a close they suddenly announced that my whole family would be sent to my hometown in the countryside to be reformed. I was totally bewildered. How could things have taken such a drastic turn?

The following day a cadre ordered me to "confess" all the valuables I had in my house. They were going to ransack the place the next day. I said I had none. He spelled it out for me: all the expensive material and clothes, good dinner sets, gold, silver, jewelry, and of course details of my bank accounts. "Would you take anything else, sir?" I asked. "No," he figured that would cover it. This same guy is the present head of security at the institute.

The next day the looters arrived in a truck and ransacked everything in sight. That same night, terrified out of his wits, my father hanged himself.

I was told about my father's death two days later. I said, "He had been in fine condition. How could he die so suddenly?" "He killed himself to escape punishment," they said. I was beside myself with anger. "What kind of crime has he ever committed?" Furious that I even dared to talk back, they told me that he had become an enemy of the masses. When I asked for permission to get his body to the crematorium, they accused me of disobedience and misbehavior. Down came another round of accusations and denunciation, followed by writing self-criticism. I wasn't allowed to go to my father's funeral. My eldest son went to the cremation but failed to bring back any ashes. In those days lots of people were dying, too many for the crematorium to handle properly. Each family just bought a cheap "ash box" and wrote down the name of the deceased. It was left by the body and if you didn't pick it up again in three days, the crematorium would get rid of it. They wouldn't even keep a record. Too, too many bodies. They just burned them in batches. In the end you'd just get back a few ashes from the whole lot. Take it or leave it. Anyway, I thought I would rake back some ashes from my father's batch and put them in my mother's tomb. That would make me feel better. However, because we had to leave the city and no one had showed up within the set time limit, we didn't get them. In '78 when I traveled back to the city to arrange my rehabilitation, I went to the crematorium. Several young girls received me and were pretty sympathetic when they heard my story. They tried hard to look for the ashes, but couldn't find them. No one kept a record of the dead.

It was September 8, 1968. I was escorted back to my house in a truck surrounded by people in red arm bands. What kind of home was it now? My father had committed suicide there, all our possessions had been looted, my wife and kids were completely terrified. They just cried and cried. When they saw me, they cried even louder. I felt so utterly miserable. A few days later, three strong young men came in a truck to escort us—my wife, our five children, and myself—back to my hometown in Hunan Province. You might be interested to know it was only less than twenty kilometers away from Mao's hometown.

I learned later that the institute sent people to my hometown with a photo of my family to arrange my settlement there. They contacted the production brigade, but the villagers said they didn't know me. As I had left home so long ago, no one recognized me. Some older people finally remembered my father.

There was nothing for us in my hometown. We weren't welcomed by the brigade as there were already too many farmers there and not enough land. One hundred thirty-two people and one hundred thirty-two mu of rice paddies. One mu per head. Far too little. There were seven members of our family and we would consume more than one thousand pounds of food each year.

But it was the government's policy to send Rightists back to the countryside. The institute people went to talk with the county officials and after a lot of trouble got us settled in. However, the brigade made some conditions. They would not be responsible for our housing and food. It was already September. Too late to get on with farming and we couldn't be given any food. How could we live? Well, our institute was a large unit and promised to give the brigade 600 yuan to build us a three-room thatched hut, and also gave each of us 6 yuan per month for the first seven months to cover living expenses. That's 294 yuan altogether. They also would get us two cubic meters of wood as building material. It wouldn't have been too bad, really, but the money went straight to the brigade for them to use to take care of us. Then they accepted us. The promised house never materialized. We were given a pigsty, which was renovated for us to live in. The building material was all taken away by the brigade cadres.

As soon as we arrived at the village, the commune militia chief and a battalion commander with two fully armed militiamen came to meet us. They told us to line up and gave us a lecture on the spot. The first thing the chief said was, "You're a landlord." Eh? I had been told I was a Rightist. How come I was being relabeled here? I found out later that in the country-side they didn't have Rightists so the ordinary peasants wouldn't know how to hate them. But "landlords"? Hey! That was a recognizable target. I didn't dare argue and in the ten years that followed I was treated as a landlord. It didn't really make any difference to me, but now my children also suffered as "children of a landlord." They weren't allowed to join the militia or take part in mass rallies. Couldn't even go to school. No studies for them until after the Cultural Revolution was over in 1976.

Back to the lecture the militia chief gave us. He continued, "You people remember these points. First: No speaking out or acting on your own ideas; second: You are not to feel as if you have been wronged; third: You must register anyone coming to see you. Report on them after they leave. . . ." He also told me to participate in the meetings for landlords, rich peasants, and other bad elements. That wasn't hard. Only once a month. We'd gather together and register ourselves. The public security chief would sit in front and shout, "You people report on your-selves!" He was always well informed. He'd sometimes list who did what on which day and yell at the people he mentioned. I was lucky. Seldom singled out by him. I'm not boasting. I performed better than anyone else there and was later appointed leader of the bad elements group. I also read newspapers for them. Most country people couldn't read, you know. I was a senior engineer so reading a paper was nothing. I also organized them in "reporting our crime" before Mao's portrait. I had previous experience. Just remember the even numbers when kowtowing. That was the key.

Food was a problem. You couldn't imagine what it was like after being used to big city living. Each person was allocated one mu of land, which could yield about 400 kilos of rice each year from the spring and winter crops. You first had to donate a certain amount to the state, then set aside seed rice and fodder rice. Anything exceeding 400 kilos you would have to sell to the state. The commune regulations only allotted 100 kilos of rice with husks per person as the basic yearly allowance. That meant about 70 kilos of rice with the husks removed. You could also earn work points to buy back extra from the commune. Most farmers could earn 500 points a year, but I was used to hard work from my days as a Rightist and could earn 600. Of course when I shared what I earned with my family, each got very little. You couldn't complain too much, though; the poor and lower middle-class peasants were starving too.

It was even harder to get hold of any money. My work points could at most get me 100 yuan or so a year. I had a big family and needed a loan from the brigade, but bad elements couldn't borrow. Still, I always managed to find a way. I found out that in the countryside the first priority was to have good relations with the local people. Then everything else would sort itself out.

I knew a little about medicine and could do acupuncture, cupping, and moxibustion.[5] Even with a bad family background, you couldn't go too wrong with that knowledge. I was extremely careful when I used the dangerous points relating to the heart. I could cure ordinary headaches, colds, and muscle pains. I never asked for any payment. Gradually I built up a good relationship with the villagers.

Another thing I noticed was that the farmers would usually raise pigs when they got a bit of money saved but that the animals were prone to disease. I learned a little from a veterinarian and got some penicillin. When the pigs were sick, I'd give them an injection behind the ear. It worked very well. I asked some city friends occasionally to send me penicillin too, the kind used for people. Very cheap. Less than 10 fen would buy a dose. Whenever people asked for me, I'd immediately go even if it was late at night or early in the morning. This helped a lot. Later on even the Party branch secretary and the security chief took a liking to me. I finally got it through their heads that I wasn't a landlord. In 1975 they held a meeting for me and announced I was no longer a landlord. This meant that I was half-rehabilitated. The villagers had only the faintest notions about Rightists, so I was treated very differently from that point on.

In the countryside there was no way to use my professional skills. You might want to help, but all they were interested in was class struggle. They just couldn't use you. Once they were building a dam. They got the earth heaped up. It had to be pressed by stone rollers with ropes attached and people pulling on the ropes. They didn't know how to do it with one guy pulling this way and another that way. They couldn't use their strength effectively. I know about this kind of work from my experience building railroads so I told them what to do. I'd call out, "Pulling up...up..." and they'd pull together at my shout. It worked, but then it suddenly dawned on the team leader, a Party member, that they couldn't listen to me. They were the poor and lower middle-class peasants and I was a class enemy. OK. So be it. I wouldn't help. But you know how it is. Capable people always want to use their talents.

In '73 the Party secretary of our commune came up with the bright idea of building a reservoir because Hua Guofeng,[6] once a prefecture Party secretary in Hunan, became well known and was promoted to the Central Committee by Mao as a result of his work on an irrigation project. Our Party secretary was going to try the same route. He organized people to start digging at the base of the mountain and to build a dam to hold the water.

I took a look and told him there weren't any water sources available there. No matter, he said, the rain would bring water. I argued that the water convergence area was too small and the rain wouldn't be sufficient. And what if it didn't rain? He insisted there was a spring near this place. I tried hard to convince him that the spring was level with the dam base and the water couldn't possibly rise to fill the reservoir. He didn't know much of anything and just stubbornly stuck to his foolish fantasy. I didn't dare argue anymore or I'd be accused of sabotage. Well, the result was that a lot of time and manpower were wasted on the useless reservoir. God knows how much. The crux of the matter is that they just wouldn't listen to you, wouldn't even let you speak, let alone use your skills. Anyone with a bit of expertise was a thorn in their sides.

I would venture to say that I never did anything harmful in my whole life. I made valuable contributions to the development of the country's railroad. Though I was made to suffer quite often, I never lost my belief in the Communist Party— they wouldn't treat innocent people like me this way forever. When I was first sent to the countryside I was only about fifty. I figured they would certainly use my skills again someday. I would wait. Even twenty years doesn't matter much. I was strong and healthy. When the Gang of Four met their downfall I was sixty. I thought that now the time had come for me to really do something for the country.

I began to arrange my own rehabilitation in 1978. Ten days after the Lunar New Year, the Number 1 Directive concerning rehabilitation was issued. I waited at home for three months but nothing happened. I'd been labeled and persecuted for more than twenty years. I couldn't wait any longer, so I went to the brigade headquarters. The brigade leader agreed to help and wrote me a letter of introduction to start with. Without that letter I couldn't get anywhere, you know. I had to follow the rules strictly. Next I went to the commune level but they were afraid to take responsibility for me and didn't want to get involved. I told them I didn't want anything written, only a stamp on the letter of introduction from the brigade. The secretary was nice enough and I finally left with a seal on my letter.

Back at the institute, the Party secretary, political affairs director, and the other chiefs and heads were my old colleagues who had been promoted. I returned to the institute on the twenty-first of May. They were quite polite to me. The Party secretary said I was being given top priority in the institute rehabilitation program. I should stay in the guest house for a while and be patient. I didn't have much else to do so I began to arrange things for myself. I went to the Municipal Organization Department, the United Front Association,[7] and other possible places. I kept pressing the institute, determined to get some results. I said to myself I would never go back home without getting what I wanted. Toward the end of August I finally got something concrete. The school would allow me to resume my position on condition that I retire right away.

You can imagine how upset I was! "I'm only sixty," I protested. "I'm still in good shape and can still work. I don't want to retire!" The Party secretary knew me well. He was my former boss. But he replied, "I know you can still work and that you've had quite a number of achievements to your credit, but to be honest with you, if you don't retire your problem cannot be solved." At that time, as you know, it was very difficult to get a city residence card. If I wanted to return to the city, I had to agree to their conditions. Otherwise my whole family and I would spend the rest of our lives out in the countryside. But for me, what good was it to resume my position without being allowed to work? I longed to return to my profession, but of course there was no other choice. My family came first.

The institute administration finally gave me a ruling on my problem. It went like this: "Comrade X's speech during the 'Antirightist' campaign was basically targeted against certain individuals on specific issues; his remarks on the 'Clique' were incorrect, but not serious enough to make him a Rightist." This conclusion was attached to my file. I was allowed to read it and told to sign if I had no objections. I leafed through my file. For heaven's sake! What kind of rubbish did they put there? All sorts of rumors and innuendoes. Not one of them could hold water. Some were just sheer fabrication. For example, a Party branch secretary who was once a field assistant under me wrote: "He collaborated with a gang of thirty people in opposition to the Party." What kind of nonsense is that? Who were those thirty people? He did it just because I didn't give him a promotion. Well, the person in charge of rehabilitation said if I would sign my problems would be settled immediately. I had to sign, had to rid myself of the Rightist label. Because of it I had suffered for over twenty years. I wrote: "I agree with the concluding part." The cadre just smiled and murmured something like, "You intellectuals are a pretty tricky lot."

All the fabrications were still left in my file and they still claimed that I had made mistakes. They were the trickiest of all. This way they would always have something to hold against me. They knew that if I got the upper hand they'd just become nobodies. That's why they would never admit they were wrong, never even give you a fair chance from the start.

Anyway, I got my label off at long last. I was on my way to tell my family the good news. Before I left for home I asked the institute for a loan. My son was getting married in the upcoming Spring Festival. In the countryside getting a wife costs a fortune. The school promised to discuss it. Well, a few days before the Spring Festival they came to see me and said that I didn't have to borrow. They would pay me back the salary they owed me according to a newly issued directive. My monthly salary had been 127 yuan. For the ten years of the Cultural Revolution it came to about 15,000 yuan altogether, but they only paid me 14,000 because they had learned from my hometown how much I had received in my years there. As for the salary they owed me from my days as a Rightist before the Cultural Revolution, they said there were no directives concerning that. I never got that money back. Ahh, the shadow of having been a Rightist has never left me. . . .

After I got my money I hurried back home. The villagers now heard that I earned over 100 yuan a month and they figured that I must be somebody important. They all came to pay their respects. Soon after, I went back to the institute to continue the process of rehabilitation. There was a long delay. I had heard rumors that there might be a freeze on. I was pretty worried so I ran around trying to get things moving. It wasn't until 1980 that the municipal government issued a directive stipulating: "All who have been wrongly charged and persecuted and sent back to their hometowns in the countryside should, in principle, return to the city with the exception of those who have married and had children there." My eldest son and daughter had already established families so they couldn't return. The rest of us, after enormous problems and constant pressure on the municipal government, did manage to come back. At first we only obtained a document allowing us to live in the city but no housing allocation. It wasn't until November that we finally got settled in. I was sixty-four then. I started to feel my age. My eyesight and hearing were going and my legs were getting useless and stiff.

From 1957 to the present, how much work could I have done for the country? How much did I do? I know. Not much. In fact, very little. My problem is like what one of my village's sayings describes as "Carrying straw on a rainy day—it becomes heavier and heavier." After I was rehabilitated, they wouldn't let me work. What's the use in that, heh? At the moment I'm helping with the accounting in the neighborhood grocery store. I feel bored at home doing nothing. At first the neighborhood people weren't sure that I could manage. But I told them, "No problem. I did budget calculations before in building railroads. Yours is simple stuff. I was a senior engineer." Would you believe they all laughed at me? I'm not sure what was so funny.

The present leading engineers in the institute design section were all trained by me. They're able to handle the big picture now. They have fresher ideas than I, but they're not as well-rounded. Not enough field experience. No practice in building new roads and bridges and long-term maintenance. Still, though, as long as they make some contributions and maybe come up with something new, I'll be very happy. How I wish I was their age and had a chance in today's world! People don't believe me when I tell them that. But it's true. I tell you. For several years I've been having dreams about designing at the drafting table again and setting up little red flags in the construction sites.

I'm not a pessismestic person. As long as I can still move about and do a few little things, I'll be happy. That's true, isn't it? But well, sometimes I get to thinking. What would it be like if by some feat of magic I could go back thirty years and start fresh? I could certainly accomplish something important. I'm sure of that much. You believe me, don't you?

The setting sun always wants to brighten the whole world with its evening glow.—F. J.

FOOTNOTES

1. The four methods defined in a directive from Chairman Mao for carrying out struggle by reasoning, namely: speaking out freely, airing views fully, holding great debates, and writing big-character posters.

2. Luo Longji and Zhang Bojun were ministry-level officials who advocated the reexamination of cases of those they believed had been wrongly accused during the previous political campaigns.

3. Still a substantial salary for the period.

4. The eighth plenum of the eighth Central Committee in the fall of 1959, which resulted in the purge of Marshal Peng Dehuai.

5. Use of Chinese mugwort in acupuncture.

6. After Mao's death in 1976 Hua Guofeng became the Premier and also assumed the posts of Chairman of the Chinese Communist Party Central Committee and Chairman of the Military Commission. In 1980 he was replaced by Zhao Ziyang as Premier, Hu Yaobang as General Secretary of the CCPCC, and Deng Xiaoping as Chairman of the Military Commission.

7. An organization of non-Communist Party members promoting the reunification of Taiwan with the mainland.

COMMANDER

NIU

TIME: *1966* 🔖 AGE: *32* 🔖 SEX: *Male*
OCCUPATION: *Cadre in charge of business in the equipment
division of a government bureau in T city*

Speaking of the ten-year Cultural Revolution, to be honest, I didn't really suffer much, and didn't get beaten up or anything. But I didn't feel any better than those who had suffered, had been beaten, searched, and humiliated. I had a weird experience, really crazy. To talk about the uncomfortable things I went through would take a couple of days, so I'll only tell you the strange part.

It all started with a nickname. You don't understand. OK. I'll start from the beginning.

I joined the revolutionary ranks quite early. When I say revolutionary ranks, I'm not talking about guerrillas fighting the Japanese, not that sort of thing. I simply mean starting work. People no longer use that expression these days, but I'm used to it.

I was in the People's Liberation Army first, teaching soldiers how to read and write. Later I became a cadre. I also studied in a technical school and did well. After that I did construction work. I kept on with my studies by myself. I'm good at many things, like technical work, management, and administration. I was also well liked. My family name is Niu, so everybody called me Little Niu. This was not the nickname that got me into trouble. During the various political campaigns and movements before the Cultural Revolution, like the "Antirightist" campaign and the Four Cleanups, I participated with enthusiasm and did very well. My one problem was my family background. My father was once a KMT army officer. That connection affected me considerably. But on the other hand, I was literally brought up in the cradle of the Communist Party. It was the Party that trained and educated me. However, I knew at heart that the Party organization didn't trust me and had misgivings about me. . . . I'm not crying about it because I feel wronged. It's hard to tell exactly why I am crying.

One year before the Cultural Revolution, I joined the Four Cleanups movement and went to the countryside. Our work group was called back after the municipal Party secretary committed suicide. By this time, the Cultural Revolution had already got going. The whole bureau was in chaos. The equipment division I worked in was a bit different from the others. It was the second largest in the bureau. It was responsible for many of the factories under the bureau. But because of the work overload, a general factory[1] incorporating several of the factories was temporarily set up before the Cultural Revolution. There hadn't been time to organize its administrative and personnel services before the Four Cleanups started. It just stopped there. With the coming of the Cultural Revolution, the general factory was totally paralyzed. Consequently all the complicated administrative issues were thrown to our division. When I came back after the Four Cleanups movement, the division was in a mess, turned upside down. The division head was taken away somewhere to be humiliated and criticized by different factories. Another cadre who knew what he was doing was also dragged away by a certain tractor factory. No one was leading the place.

As I was older, more experienced, and educated, the bureau head put me in temporary charge. Back then, no one cared about business. Some were afraid of losing their positions and privileges. Some wanted to gain some power. Otherwise I would never have been chosen. I was an ordinary cadre and faced with these problems, I was at a total loss. I was up to my ears in work, but I could hardly keep things under control.

At this time, all the work units were busy setting up their so-called rebellion teams. Most divisions in our bureau also followed suit. People felt unsafe without belonging to some sort of organization. Only our division was at a standstill. Our chief was not available and other cadres were taken away. I became the focus of attention. People asked me to take the lead. But I'm a timid person and afraid of making trouble. Also, as I said, my family background did not help. So I tried to stall and avoid doing anything. Better to stay quiet than to move.

In accordance with the Sixteen-Point Directive, revolutionary committees were elected all over the place, as in the Paris Commune where each person had the right to vote. Our bureau's revolutionary committee consisted of four members. The former party committee office head became the director and I was elected one of the three deputy directors. I felt greatly honored and fortunate. If not for the Paris Commune—style election, how could I, with my background, have been chosen?

The committee's target was the "monsters." The director and the other two deputy directors took charge of the burning, smashing, and fighting because they all had good backgrounds like the Red Guards. But they were not experienced in professional administrative work. So I led a dozen cadres in nonpolitical work. I felt the movement this time was much stronger than those that had occurred before. I knew there was a lot more to it than it appeared on the surface. I must learn the lessons of history. My family background told me I must be careful. Otherwise I'd be in trouble. I buried myself in my work. But it wouldn't do if you ignored political struggle— you'd be accused of being disloyal to Chairman Mao. So I found myself a job receiving the Red Guards.

It wasn't so easy. Bunches of Red Guards came one after another from all over the country. Some were polite enough, but others were extremely rude. We had to take care of them —give them food and lodging—no matter how they behaved. We got blankets, sheets, or straw for them and bought them sweaters, cotton-padded jackets, and other warm clothes. They ate and stayed without paying. The higher-ups issued a directive calling on people to support the Red Guards. It was a hard job. The young revolutionaries were not so easy to please. Our division had to move several times to give our office to the Red Guards. Finally we had to move into the conference room of the bureau director.

At this time, other divisions had already set up rebellion teams. Only ours was an exception. This gave people the impression that we were not revolutionary enough. We were suspected of having some resentment or complaints against the Cultural Revolution. It put a kind of invisible pressure on us, so

I came up with an idea. We started two hours of political study every afternoon, reading newspaper articles, documents, and editorials in the "Two Papers One Journal".[2] We also studied Mao's works, sang songs based on his quotations, the "International" and "The Sea Voyage Depends Upon the Helmsman."[3] There was a popular slogan then: "If you are not revolutionary, you must be counterrevolutionary." One former bureau director asked me, "Why are you people so conservative? Everybody has a team. Aren't you afraid that others would use it against you?" Another old cadre in charge of professional work, a nice old guy, advised me in secret that I'd better start taking some action. I thought about it. I found a leaflet somewhere, a declaration by a rebellion team of some sort. I kept their wording but changed the signatures. I also named us the East-Is-Red-Rebellion Team. I used the mimeograph machine to print lots of them. The former bureau director even gave me a hand. Then we distributed them. This was the start of our organization. Since our team was the last one to be set up, the whole bureau was now "Red" all over.

In fact, this didn't solve our problems. The whole bureau and all the affiliated factories under it had already divided into two main factions.

My division had the largest number of people in the place, in charge of dozens of different factories. Some of the factories had no leaders. We had to take care of them directly. We were believed to be the most powerful division. Altogether we had thousands of workers. So the situation was that both factions wanted to win us over.

My thought then was that I had to be extremely careful not to get involved in any trouble, not to get caught by a repeat of the tactics of the "Antirightist" campaign in 1957.[4] The organization I helped to set up was only a blind. Movements were always temporary. I had to lead our people through this time safely. No matter what, we would not be more revolutionary than others. Not be too conspicuous, not get into any fighting or trouble. Not take sides with either faction.

Before we got our own rebellion team going, we had been watching the revolution of the rebellion teams from the outside, and now we were seeing them from the inside. To tell the truth, though people were quoting Mao's call to "Pay attention to state affairs," they were in fact thinking and doing something else. During this movement, some people were fighting for personal interests; others were like me, trying to remain quiet to protect themselves. People were no longer as trusting and sincere as they had been in '57. Political movements had taught people to be cleverer, more cautious, and more deceitful.

I only did some unimportant things that didn't entail any danger. I did things like keeping an eye on the "monsters," organizing their political studies, and going out to put up big-character posters. "A gentleman only moves his lips, not his fists." I didn't join in any fighting. Actually, there wasn't much violence in our bureau.

The two factions in the bureau were the result of personal conflicts. Political differences were only a convenient pretext. The two sides were each led by one bureau leader. Everybody was clear about the distinction and it became clearer once the Cultural Revolution broke out. One group consisted of the old-timers and the other of the people who had joined the bureau later, with the new leader. Most of them were administrative cadres. People on both sides were experienced in various kinds of struggles. They were good at sneak attacks and backstabbing. Under-the-counter sorts of things. They could quarrel their heads off one minute and the next have lunch together, chatting and laughing. So it was mostly like this. Not too bad really. At least no bloodletting, no one at each other's throats. Later, the Great Alliance[5] was not very hard to achieve. Dozens of different groups just put their titles together at the bureau entrance.

I was mainly in charge of production. "Promoting Production," it was called. It was the safest job of all. Even when they finally settled all the accounts, they wouldn't pick on the people who did the work. We kept on working and didn't stop even when thousands of cadres were sent off to the countryside. I thought I was safe at last.

But the problem is when you don't ask for trouble, trouble looks for you, and it found me.

One day a rebellion team chief came to see me. He had a notebook with him. It was probably around '67. He said "This book was found during a search of a municipal leader's house on the thirtieth of May. It records things said about you when our bureau chief reported his work." I looked at it and was shocked. It said my father was a KMT army commander. I was really upset. It was bullshit. How could I become the son of a KMT commander all of a sudden?

Later on, after all the different factions were allied, I once asked this guy about it in front of a crowd. Another guy from the construction division joined in. "I know all about it," he said. "A couple of years ago, one comrade in our office said that the KMT commander Niu mentioned in Ma Ji's[6] comic routine was Little Niu's father. He was kidding. But it was later reported to the division head and it became truth. He in turn reported it to the bureau chief. That was how it happened."

Everybody just laughed after this guy's explanation. I was quite angry that the chief used it against me. I demanded an apology from him. He was very arrogant because he had a backup. His brother was a sort of high-up cadre in Beijing. He refused to admit he had done wrong. Instead he insulted me: "You son of a bitch! Who are you to question me? I'm sure you'll retaliate when the KMT comes back . . ." I was furious and I struck him on the neck. I didn't slap his face because he was wearing a pair of glasses. I was also standing a bit away from him so in fact only my fingers touched him. But from that moment on, my nickname became Commander Niu.

The nickname first meant my father, then it became me. I didn't really take it too seriously. It was only a joke after all. I sometimes even felt proud of it. I was in charge of production and quite capable in administration. By calling me that name, people actually showed me some respect. So I just accepted it. If someone phoned, he simply said, "Commander Niu," and everybody would know he was looking for me. It was like this at first in the bureau, then it spread to some of the factories. People who didn't know my real name all knew there was a Commander Niu in the equipment division.

Later, when cadres were sent to the grass roots to be workers or go to cadres' schools[7] or transferred to other places, I was assigned to work in a factory, and my nickname went with me. It had become a term of endearment. Whenever someone addressed me by it, I'd feel we were very close. It should just stop at that, right? But it didn't.

In 1976, when the Cultural Revolution ended and the check-ups got going, somehow, I don't know how, the factory people all got to believe that I was the "Commander" in the bureau, the chief of all the rebellion teams. Imagine how I felt about that. I'm not sure which son of a bitch spread the rumor. But this time it wasn't a joke. Everybody was convinced of it.

The guy I gave a love tap to now insisted that I beat him. I consequently became a "smasher and grabber"[8] member. I was constantly being investigated. My promotion and grading were both affected. Even my proposal for reforms was given the cold shoulder.

You see, just a nickname, started as a joke, has made me

guilty of some crimes during the Cultural Revolution. I really should have stopped it from the beginning. If someone used my nickname, I should have cleared things up then and there. I really should have done it.

Another thing was some photos. Once during a public accusation meeting criticizing people in power, the municipal deputy Party secretary was in the dock as an accomplice. But the person who was holding him was puny. The guy in charge called on me. I was big and strong, and so I did it. Some photos were taken. These photos were later dug up. They became one more evidence of my crimes during the Cultural Revolution. It got added to my nickname. I just have such rotten luck.

After the Cultural Revolution, the bureau I had worked in set up a new governing body. The older people, the ones on my side, had left and the others all tried to avoid dealing with any problems. They wanted to shift the responsibility to those who were no longer working there. The result was no one tried to defend me or explain for me. Instead, they hoped I would be singled out and blamed. Therefore the "Rebel Commander" label was accepted as truth. It really made my life miserable. One investigation after another. They wouldn't talk it out with me face to face. They just did it behind my back. They couldn't get results, but still they wouldn't give up.

Each time when the checkups were getting under way, some well-intentioned friends would phone me not to show up at the bureau. They all behaved as if I did have some things to hide. If I went to ask about it, everybody would say, "Who is investigating you? Don't be so nervous. Do you have something to hide?" It really put me on the spot. I couldn't even go to the bureau to get business done.

Back in the factory, I was at loose ends. No one said anything to me, but everyone assumed I was in trouble. It went on like this for several years.

The year before last, the Municipal Party Organization Department formally notified me that after lots of investigations, my problem had been clarified. Well, I didn't beat anybody up and I wasn't a smasher and grabber. Last year the city discipline inspection committee people talked to me. They said, "Your life hasn't been easy these years. Your promotion to factory deputy manager was delayed too. After repeated investigations, your status is now clear." At long last my problem was resolved.

The municipal people also said my nickname didn't matter much and there was no need to explain it to anyone. They didn't formally file the case, so there was no question of rehabilitation. Now people who don't know the whole story still keep calling me Commander Niu. Others have stopped. Perhaps they realize it doesn't do me any good. Pretty ridiculous, eh?

Life's absurdities are stranger than fiction.—F. J.

FOOTNOTES

1. A general factory consists of several factories combined into one under one administration.

2. Colloquial name for the *People's Daily, PLA Daily,* and *Red Flag Journal.* They carried the government's policy guidelines and collectively reflected the views of the Party.

3. A popular song eulogizing Mao.

4. The "Antirightist" campaign of 1957 cracked down on many who had criticized the Party just previously, when such criticism had been officially encouraged.

5. Movement in 1967 to eliminate factionalism and the violence that characterized the early days of the Cultural Revolution.

6. Well-known stage performer.

7. According to Mao's May Seventh Directive (1968), schools were to be set up all over the country in late 1968 for cadres to do manual labor and ideological reeducation.

8. Refers to those who were involved in violence and fighting during the Cultural Revolution.

A
MODERN
ROUGE
ET NOIR

TIME: *1966* ❧ AGE: *17* ❧ SEX: *Male*
OCCUPATION: *High school student in T city*

What I'm going to tell you is something I can't talk about to my family or to my friends. Not even my best friends. It's my inner torment. Not the immediate sharp kind of pain, but a very deep thing, something you can't get rid of. I don't understand myself why I came to tell you about it.

My total flaw was my bad family background. I started to feel it when I was in high school. It was around '64 and '65. I was a senior. I was a hard-working student, politically progressive and close to the Party organization. I didn't know what it was about me that repelled those with good family backgrounds. They all tried to avoid me. Not like mice running away at the sight of cats, but like people fleeing from plague. They even looked down on me. I didn't know what was happening. Naturally I became closer to those few students with similar family background problems. Sometimes we complained among ourselves. Because of that, we were all labeled "black gangsters" in 1966. I'm not going into details about that. I don't want to complain. I'm only talking about what happened to me.

My family was living in quite a decent apartment. Suddenly, for no reason, the local government ordered us to move out. My grandparents and parents were timid people, so we obeyed without a word. After that, some sort of high-ranking official moved in. This brought me under strong pressure, a kind of political as well as psychological pressure. It showed the political status of my family.

When the Cultural Revolution began, everything fell into place. My family was one of the first in the city to be ransacked.

I later found out that it was my mother's ignorance that started the ransacking. Both my grandfather and father were working in banks. They were well-known capitalists. At that time all the funds capitalists had in the banks were frozen. You couldn't withdraw anything. It was called "money made by exploitation." All the names of capitalists were listed just outside the banks. My mother didn't know about that. She went to get some money out. The bank clerks immediately called the Red Guards. They showed up in no time at my home and started to search and ransack our apartment.

I heard about this and didn't dare go back. I went to see a close classmate and asked him to go back home with me. He was too scared. His father was a clerk or something and he wasn't sure what would be done to people with his background.

He said, "Your neighbors all know me, and that will bring trouble to my family as well." In the end, I went home by myself. From a distance, I could see big-character posters everywhere near my home. My mother was being denounced outside the house. Lots of noisy people packing the place. Things were smashed and burnt. Smoke was still in the air. I was only seventeen that year and had never seen anything like that. I didn't dare go any closer. That night I stayed outside, walking back and forth in the street the whole night. I had no idea how my mother and grandparents survived that experience. My younger brother was handicapped. I was most worried about him.

The next day, I went to see the Red Guards responsible for ransacking my family. I figured I'd take anything from them: insults, criticism, and everything else. I was going to beg them to allow me to go home to have a look. My other brothers were living in other cities. Only that handicapped brother was living with my parents. I had always taken care of him since he was small. I taught him how to read and write and draw pictures, and told him about life. We cared about each other very much.

One Red Guard was decent. He took me home. I glanced over the rooms from the corridor. Red Guards were standing everywhere, searching for things. No sign of my family. Lots of things were in shreds, smashed and torn. The things I treasured the most were my stamp collection and my correspondence with Soviet friends. In the early sixties, you know, we were encouraged to have contacts with the Russians. Those cherished things were lying on the floor everywhere but now they were no longer important to me. The only thing left in me was the desire to survive. I forgot about everything, even my hunger. I asked the Red Guards to let my brother go with me. Leaving my family was something the Red Guards didn't object to. I was going to break with my family. It was revolutionary action. And also my brother was still quite young and a cripple. So they agreed to let us go. I took two bed sheets with me and we went to live in my school dormitory. Before we left, they gave me five yuan and some food coupons. I had asked for them. I was very grateful when they handed them to me. I was not sure how long the money could last. Because my family was quite well-off, we had never had to know the real value of money.

My brother and I lived on the five yuan for over a month. My school didn't allow us to stay on. Our apartment had been sealed up. My parents moved in with my mother's family. Their home had been searched and sealed too. My parents just blocked off a tiny area with a piece of cloth in the corridor. They found some wooden boards to use as a bed. When I went to see my mother, her hair had been cut and shaved by the Red Guards, white and black. Her appearance made the deepest impression on me. My father's parents were now living in a tiny place on another block. The Red Guards asked my brother and me to stay there.

The five yuan the Red Guards gave me caused some misunderstanding between me and my family. I bought some snacks with the money for my brother but didn't give any to my grandparents. They were just watching us eating. They told this to my uncles and aunts. But how would I dare to give money to them? It was from the Red Guards.

At this time, my mother didn't have any income. I'm not sure how she managed to live. I admit I just didn't dare have anything to do with my family. I couldn't afford to care about them. Imagine. I was only seventeen and caught in this situation for the first time in my life. I simply didn't know what to do. My only concern was to look out for my brother and myself. This misunderstanding still seems to exist between me and my family even now.

When I used up the money, I braced myself to ask for more from the Red Guards. They would give me some each time and I'd spend it on my brother and myself. I was not to have anything to do with the rest of the family. I had no choice.

Even when I was in such a position, I didn't totally resign myself to it. I wanted to live and survive and get a place for myself in society. I deserved to enjoy things just like everybody else. Some of my classmates were very cocky. Why should I suffer? I wasn't dumber or weaker than them, was I? It was all because of my inherited family background. I hated my family connection. I even started to hate my own parents and my ancestors but I wouldn't just let them crush me. I couldn't swallow that. I wanted to keep on struggling and prove myself someday.

In 1968, when the Going to the Countryside Movement started, I volunteered to go. I told the school authorities that my family couldn't support me financially anymore. I went to Inner Mongolia in the North, a place about twenty kilometers from the border, a desolate place. But suddenly I felt I'd thrown away the burden of my family background at last. However, my team leader told the locals about my situation later. He even reported to the brigade Party branch people. Now everybody knew about me again. What can you do in such a situation? I just worked hard. That was the only way out for me.

Farmers are different from city people. Working hard means a lot to them. If you're a hard worker, a good farmhand, you won't starve. They'll respect you too. You are judged by your ability to survive. I managed to do double the amount of work others did. I worked like crazy, with my family tree still pressing down on my shoulders. I wanted to get a foothold in the countryside. At the end of each year, everybody would go for visits home. They asked me to go too, but I refused. I told them I didn't have a home. When we got our payments each year, I always got the most—27 yuan. I'd keep ten and send the rest back home.

In the brigade I'd do whatever I was asked no matter how hard it was. In the middle of the winter, they'd ask me to post slogans on the walls or to write them out. The freezing cold wind would be blowing hard coming down from the northwest. I had only a light PLA uniform on me. Too cold to open your hands, but I had to hold a brush to paint the slogans: "Long Live Mao Zedong Thought," "Socialism Is Good," and things like that. It was ironic. Even when I was feeling down no one ever lent me warm clothes. I often wondered why there seemed to be no place for me even in this Mongolian wilderness. I'm not complaining. I'm just telling you the truth.

Farmers are generally honest. They appreciate real down-to-earth things. After three years there, they got me to teach in the local school. At this time, people among us started to be chosen to go back to the cities. I knew my place. No need to try to get chosen. It would be useless. I wasn't qualified. In the first two batches, all the people from good family backgrounds went. Only girls and people with some disabilities were left behind. In the third batch, our team leader, the one I just mentioned, was left out in the cold. His father was a sort of small business-man, a store owner, and something about him was not clarified. Unexpectedly I had my lucky break. I was assigned to work for a railroad administration in a large city.

I started off as a transport worker at a railroad station. Now my situation was much better. My job was backbreaking but no one knew about my family. I mingled with my fellow workers, working, eating, and sleeping just like them. We got along quite well. I could finally live like everybody else, without that kind of distance.

One day, though, we were going to dig air raid shelters. First we lined up on the platform. Then the chief said those with bad family backgrounds are going to carry the rocks from the hills and the others do the digging. Next they were going to roll call those with family problems. I had a sinking feeling in my stomach. My face turned red and I tried to lower my head as much as possible. I was the first to be called. I had to stand up front. Now my secret was out. I was finished here once again. No hope for me for the rest of my life. No escape from the shadow of my family background.

Up in the hills, we first used explosives to get rocks out and then tied up the rocks with steel wire to carry them down to the trains on shoulder poles. I had worked in the countryside before, so that was no problem for me. I only felt my family background pressing me down, much heavier than the rocks. Almost too much for me to keep going.

Later on I was assigned to teach in the railroad middle school. I was a high school graduate so teaching was no big deal for me. In the school I carefully toed the line: Always keep quiet during political meetings and find a corner to sit in. I knew I had no right to speak. I knew too well what my position was. I should feel grateful just to be allowed to exist. But whenever I could use my abilities, I'd always try my best. Sometimes I had conflicting feelings: At first I'd feel helpless, frustrated, and ready to give up. But then I'd begin to really resent the treatment I got, resent my fate. I wanted my value to be recognized and I wanted to build up my self-respect. It's not easy to do this when you're being humiliated. Something like putting up a pillar of mud in the middle of a roaring torrent.

About that time I got to know two girls. One was a little extroverted and the other was the opposite. They were good friends too, like sisters to each other.

The first girl was real talkative and intelligent. She was capable too. I got along with her just great. She came from the same city as me. I was totally amazed when she told me she lived in the same apartment my family had been kicked out of. Her parents were the high-ranking officials. It was a coincidence and almost melodramatic. She was once a Red Guard herself and a chief of some sort too, doing the ransacking and searching stuff. I never dreamed I'd make friends with a person from a genuine Red family, let alone go steady with a Red Guard. It was funny in a way.

Now I started to think seriously. I was a hopeless case. Anybody could get away with calling me a prick. This time I'd show them all how I'd marry one of the "five red categories."[1] I'd looked forward to the results. Her family would definitely oppose it, but the stronger their opposition, the more determined I would be. To tell the truth, I wanted to do it for revenge. I was going to see how Red people would treat me then. During all those years, I was pretty depressed. I knew I was going to explode sooner or later and might become a counterrevolutionary or something. I found this way to get it out. Not very decent really, but now I was going to become a relative of those Red Categories. Let them sit back and watch how I'd do it.

It was really a marriage of Red and Black, a kind of hybrid.

As for my relations with the girl, I liked her. She was clever and straightforward. Especially because she made friends with a person like me, I felt very comforted and grateful to her. But of course all this had to do with her difficult situation at the moment too. It was her parents' turn to be criticized. She was alone in this miserable place, far away from home, no family or friends around. Naturally she was lonely. We also enjoyed each other's company. Another thing was that the other girl was chasing me. I didn't like that one, but I pretended to. This made the first girl pretty jealous. It helped a lot in getting our relationship going. I did all this on purpose. I needed to do it. I wanted revenge and, at the same time, to get myself established in society.

My parents didn't believe such a marriage could last. We weren't compatible: her Red and me Black. Just too different. Problems would certainly arise in the future. Her family was dead set against it too, but I told them, "I insist on visiting even if you object. Maybe my family background isn't good enough, but I'm your future son-in-law." Though I put up a good front, I did feel pretty bad inside. Am I a human being or not? Why don't I have the right to marry like anybody else?

The first time I saw her mother, I called her Mom. She didn't answer me. I figured no matter how she reacted, I'd go through with it anyway.

After we got married, things started to change for me. Very strange. In my work unit, people began to treat me like somebody. I couldn't figure it, I was still the same guy. But in their eyes, I was no longer "just a prick." The purpose of this marriage was to move up in the world, you know, get a better job and go to college; I didn't go through with it just to enjoy all the comforts and to be able to do whatever I wanted. Before, I was good for nothing. I couldn't go to college, couldn't join the Party, couldn't even speak at meetings. I was not trusted politically to do anything. My marriage changed all that. Very soon after we married, I got transferred back to the city with my wife. My position changed immediately. My own family could never have gotten such good connections. My old schoolmates? I've noticed those with family background problems are still not making it. Now I'm much better off.

I took advantage of my wife's family connections and I managed to go to college and join the Party. Everybody seemed to have forgotten about my family problem. I wasn't a bad-category person anymore, but I wasn't really a good one either. I was something in between. I got fairly decent treatment. Before, a person like me wouldn't even have dreamed of joining the Party. The mere mention of it would have made people laugh their heads off. Think about it. In the past, no matter how I suffered, no matter how hard I worked, I would never have gotten this far.

My wife's family had never accepted me and my parents didn't get along with her very well either. She didn't think much of my mother, too proud to even talk to her. But personally, I was satisfied—I got what I wanted.

Later on, things began to change between us. Especially after the Cultural Revolution. As her family situation improved, her moods became more complex. She once told me she regretted marrying me. She renewed her relations with her old friends and classmates, the ones from high-ranking officials' families. She started comparing me with them and felt ashamed of having a husband like me. Some of her friends have either gone abroad or become upper-level cadres. I have only two things going for me that she can find some solace in. I'm now in charge of my work unit, and I'm also a college graduate so I've got the education to deal with normal social functions. But when it comes to the higher circles of her friends, I am not good enough. Fortunately, we have a child. Children are the strongest bond between husband and wife. Yeah, that's so, but I guess we still do have lots of friction and conflicts, especially when she's in one of her superior moods because of her family status.

I think I've reached a dead end in what I'm doing. The best years of my life were wasted during the Cultural Revolution. I can't achieve much in my profession. The only chance left open to me is the political path. But even in this, those with better family backgrounds have a big advantage over me. I tried to get to the top on my own, but you can't succeed in what you are doing without strong family backing. Now, I don't want to use my wife's family's influence. Even if I do, it's only indirect. It doesn't produce any substantive results. At the beginning, I benefited from her family but now it doesn't mean much. After all, I'm not inherently Red, no Red roots. I know another fellow. His father is head of the Public Security Bureau. He managed pretty well and became quite a high official. But a person can't get anywhere if he doesn't have the right connections. No backup. On the surface, this family of mine looks all right, but once someone gets to know my history, they'll start thinking twice about it.

I'm disgusted talking about this. Let's talk about something else, hey?

"A twisted love means a twisted life." —F. J.

FOOTNOTE

1. Refers to the children of workers, peasants, cadres, soldiers, and revolutionary martyrs.

A
YOUNG
GIRL
LOST

TIME: *1974* 🦋 AGE: *32* 🦋 SEX: *Male*
OCCUPATION: *Teacher in an art and design school in T city*

F irst of all, I want you to know I've got something different to tell you. This story is not about myself. It's about someone else, but I saw it with my own eyes. I did suffer pretty badly during those years. I almost went out of my mind. The reason I'm not telling you my own story isn't that it hurts too much to talk about it but that others' sufferings are sometimes easier to remember. Especially this story. I really tried to find this person again, but I didn't get anywhere. In China, with one billion people around, it's not so easy to find a person like her, no matter how hard you try....

I think it was in 1974. I was teaching drawing in an arts and crafts school. The spring of that year, we were going to take the students to do some fieldwork. It was still a little chilly. Another teacher was going with me. He was teaching flower painting and I handled scenery painting. He first went to Heze, home of the peonies in Shangdong, and then planned to meet me on Mt. Taishan. Spring's a good time for peonies.

I went to Taishan to wait for them. I stayed in a small hotel near Zhongtianmen Gate. The scenery was fantastic. The mountain peaks were steep and dangerous and the valleys deep and mysterious. You could take a stroll to the west and see different sides of the mountain. Unfortunately, it was raining at the time and spring rain is always endless. So every day, I just sat there in front of the window painting rain scenes. Meanwhile, I was patiently awaiting my students. But they didn't show up on time. I heard it rained even harder in Heze. Peonies, as a rule, would certainly wither in the heavy rain, and maybe the students had returned to school. No phone up there in the mountains. A letter would take days to get through. Usually you had to ask the workers to deliver your mail up and down the mountains. I was stuck there. The rain was getting heavier and heavier, but the scenery was improving too. The sound of water rushing in the streams could be heard everywhere. Waterfalls appeared too, something rare this early in the season. Well, let's skip the nice part, because the rest of my story is really pretty depressing.

I was trapped in the mountains for ten days. On the eleventh, the sky started to clear up and the clouds disappeared. I decided to hurry down. I didn't have too much money with me. If I didn't leave, I'd really be in trouble if the rain picked up again. When I got to the foot of the mountain, it had completely cleared. I bought a ticket back at the Tai'an railway station. The train was due at three o'clock the same afternoon. I had some simple food and found a sunny place to wait. The waiting room was too damp and miserable from the constant rain. I found a spot near the wall and rolled up a big rock to sit on. Near me a couple of other passengers were waiting too. Some were dozing off, wrapped in huge cotton jackets, others were playing cards. An old man was selling things in a small stall. My spot wasn't too noisy and it was relatively clean. No flies bothering you. Still too cold for them. Looking up, you could see the magnificent mountains rearing up before you. Quite awesome, like waves upon waves. I didn't have anything to do, so I took out my drawing board and was going to start sketching. Then I sensed someone approaching me.

I looked up and saw a girl in front of me. She was dressed in very shabby clothes. Her hair was a mess, covering most of her face. Her head was lowered. I couldn't see her clearly. She seemed to be coming straight toward me. Before I realized what was going on, she suddenly knelt down before me. I was taken totally by surprise. Anybody else would have been too. I asked, "What's the matter?" She didn't reply or move. People nearby were surprised too. I tried again, "Are you in trouble?" The girl didn't lift her head, but I could see tears rolling down her cheeks and dropping to the ground. She didn't cry out loud. Only a muffled sound escaped her throat. I couldn't stand this, so I just kept asking, "Sister, what's wrong with you? If you need money, I can help you. I've bought my ticket and I can give the rest to you. Please do tell me what's wrong. I can certainly help." The guy wrapped in the jacket, a discharged young soldier, spoke up too: "Listen, he's talking to you. Don't just cry. I can help you too if you just tell us what's wrong. We may be able to solve your difficulties. Just tell us. We can help you. Do trust us..." His accent and way of speaking told me he was a typical Shandong guy, a righteous type. His words

could fill you with warmth. The others also began to encourage
her to open up. Finally she lifted her head. She had fine features, though they were bathed in tears. She looked pale and
her eyes were heavily shadowed. Her face was a picture of
misery. She must have run into great trouble. She finally started
to tell us her story. She spoke simply, but each word pierced my
heart like an arrow. . . .

She was from Jinan, the capital city of Shandong. Her father
was supposed to be politically problematic, but he died when
she was still very young. Her mother brought her up all by
herself. Her dead father's legacy was a heavy burden. The
mother was too outspoken and once said something in defense
of her father. She was arrested as a result. Because of this, all
the girl's relatives and friends stayed away from her. She had to
live on her own, mainly by selling the family belongings, and
she was often cheated. Her home was nearly empty. When the
Going to the Countryside Movement started, she volunteered
and was sent to a village in the areas in Tai'an mountain. Her
mother later died in prison. She was not even allowed to go
back to pay a last visit. Instead she just received a notification
after the work unit disposed of the body. She was not allowed
to have any emotional bonds with her parents, but she was
politically bound to them.

She continued to tell us her story: "The villagers and city
kids were all mean to me. The brigade saw me as a member of
the "four bad elements."[1] I had a bad kidney problem. Sometimes I could hardly stand up. They kept giving me hard work.
If you could work hard, you'd be all right, but very often I had
to go hungry. Nobody even lent me anything. I couldn't live
there anymore. I ran away from there. I felt I was finally free.
But then I realized I have no place to go. If I go back to the
city, nobody would bother to take care of me. And if I return

to the brigade, there's no way they'll let me off easy. At the very best I'll be labeled an 'escapist' from the revolutionary ranks. It will get even worse for me in future.

"I met a guy at the station here. He's a salesman from Xinjiang. He told me he was a Beijing student assigned to work there. His parents are in Beijing. He's over thirty. Quite a sympathetic guy. He said he'll take me to Xinjiang if I marry him. I have no idea what to do. Please help me and decide for me. Please tell me what to do. . . ."

I was totally stunned. How can a young girl ask a stranger to decide on her marriage? But in those days things like this did happen. Think about it from her point of view: She was homeless, nowhere to go, no one to turn to. So young and inexperienced. Who else could she talk to? She must have noticed me and decided that I was an educated person and not a bad guy. But this posed a difficult problem for me. I had to decide her future and fate. I might show her a way out or throw her into a blind alley. I often thought I had good ideas and my friends frequently asked my opinion when they were in trouble. Now I felt I was at a total loss for the first time. I turned to the discharged soldier for help. He was staring at me. His righteous air seemed to have disappeared without a trace. I had to say something. It wasn't something to pass off lightly. But she had put her entire fate in my hands. The responsibility was too heavy!

I couldn't make up my mind. I was at a loss for words, but the girl was looking at me very expectantly. It was as if no one but me could have the final solution and she'd accept whatever I said. The salesman was leaving. She had to live and eat and have a place to sleep. Not so easy to go begging. Class struggle was still strong everywhere, and no one dared to give food to a stranger. I had to help her. What I had to deal with were her basic problems of eating and sleeping on the one hand and her life and future fate on the other.

Out of desperation, I suddenly had an idea. "Ask the Xinjiang man to come here. We'll talk to him first before making any decisions."

The former soldier looked at me and seemed to agree. The girl's face brightened at my words and she left to get the salesman. The rest of us squatted down and decided to bombard the Xinjiang salesman with hard questions. We wouldn't let the girl be destroyed by him.

A few minutes later, the girl came back with a man. He was about the same height as she was. His legs were short and bowed. He was wearing a big blue cotton jacket and carrying a black briefcase. His skin was dark and rough from working outdoors. His eyes were wide open and alert. A typical salesman type. He looked over forty. Before we stood up, he squatted down just opposite us. Next he took out a pack of cigarettes, handed me one and threw one to each of the others. This was the common practice among salesmen. We were about to refuse but he said with a smile that showed his cracked teeth, "Drinks and smokes are for everyone." He certainly was a salesman.

Before I could begin to examine him closely, his gaze already pierced each of us as if we were transparent. He was too alert. I began to feel a bit worried. I asked, "Which part of Xinjiang are you from?" He immediately produced a letter of introduction from his pocket. He shook off the tobacco on it and handed it to me. Next he took out his little red work identity card. His photo was on it with a red official stamp. He was from Urümqi, a place called the Red Flag Printing House. He was here to buy some printing machines. Nothing suspicious about his identity. We relaxed a little. Each of us examined his letter and card without knowing what to say next. We felt stupid.

He started again, "We are all strangers. Whether you believe what I said or not, it's up to you. I'd like to remind you of one thing. The girl was a stranger to me too. I accepted what she told me as the truth. I'm not dragging her with me. I was waiting for my train and saw she was crying there, sobbing very hard. I thought maybe she needed money and I was going to give her some, but she told me her escape story. Under the skin, we are all human. Right? I sympathize very much with her. I came from Beijing originally. My family lives in No. 117 Caodacang near Xizhiman Gate. My parents and a sister are still living there. I went to Xinjiang ten years ago. I was a lathe operator. The factory people were impressed by my work and saw that I was good at running around and public relations so they asked me to be their salesman. Pretty hard job, hey. I'm not married yet. You people have no idea about what Xinjiang is like. The city women there mostly came with their husbands. Single women all try to marry out of the place. The local girls? Well, we can't get along with them. So you see it's impossible for me to get a wife from the city. No girl from the central cities wants to go to that godforsaken place. I couldn't even get a cripple or a blind woman to marry me and go there. That's why I'm still single. But don't assume I have to have a wife. Single men like me enjoy our freedom and fun. And I'm used to living by myself. Marriage was the furthest thing from my mind until I met this girl. I felt that she was really pathetic, had no one to turn to. I only want to help and the only way I can help her is to take her back with me. But I can't just take a girl to live with me without any justification, can I? I won't do that sort of thing. I can't just tell everybody she was my sister. They would say, 'What sister is that? You never mentioned a younger sister in any of your registration forms.' Right? But I can't just leave her like this either. To be honest, it's not so simple to take care of a wife nowadays, don't you agree? She has no residence card, no food ration. Can't live no matter where she goes. It's only me that's willing to take her on. I've been in my profession for quite a few years and have a few connections back home. It's not impossible to get a card for her and it's not as strict in Xinjiang as it is here. . . .

"I'm saying all this just to tell you not to worry. Since I want to marry her, I won't let her down. I'm thirty-six and she's only twenty. I'm a lot older. How can an adult mistreat a little girl? If I treat her well, she'll surely not be bad to me. Just now she said she had to talk to somebody and found you people. Now you please think it over and decide whether it'll be all right or not. If it's yes, I'll take her; if not, I'll get lost. I don't have a guilty conscience at all. I just said, I'm not the type that has to marry. I'm just sympathetic. And to be honest, I'm also doing this because she's an honest person. She'll bring me luck, I guess. I've said so much and opened my heart to you. Now you decide. Since she trusts you, I trust you too. That's all. Your turn now. . . ."

The other people all turned to me. The guy sounded reasonable and honest enough. No one had anything to say. What could I do? I looked at the letter and his card over and over again. The more I looked at them, the most helpless I felt. The girl and the salesman didn't look compatible, one so quiet and innocent, the other experienced almost to the point of being slick. Their age difference was significant, too. If I say no, then after the man leaves, what can the girl do? All of us have to go our own way. She will be left here with no food and no shelter, worse than a stray cat. None of us could take her home. Food was one problem, but there were lots more. Which one of us could have a spare room or a bed for her? What could we do about her residence card? Without it, you'd be charged with hiding people illegally.

I didn't know what to do. I turned to the girl finally and

asked, "What do you think?" She wouldn't raise her head and she wouldn't reply. Ah well, how stupid of me. She came to ask me for my opinion in the first place. I faced the salesman. "If she has no objections, and she goes with you, you must take good care of her no matter what happens. Try to look at things from her position. A girl like her, with no parents or relatives, goes to such a faraway place with you, travels thousands of miles. If . . . if you mistreat her, who else can she turn to?"

The salesman immediately dismissed my admonitions with a sweeping gesture. "Don't talk like that. You said you're concerned about her. I'm even more so. But you only say it with words. I'm ready to take her back and feed her. Or how about you taking her with you? I'd really admire you if you did. Give it a try. You won't, eh? I'm not trying to offend you. I simply don't want you to misinterpret my good intentions. Think about it. I have to pay for her train fare. How much is that going to cost me? She obviously can't work immediately in such poor shape. I think she'll only be good for household chores. I'll have to feed her and clothe her. But I won't have any complaints about that. She'll be my wife. Who else will look after her if not me? I'm certainly not taking her back just to quarrel and fight. Am I so fed up with life or what? Why should I look for trouble and sacrifice my bachelor's freedom? Moreover, think about me. I'm pushing forty. I want to have children and start a family. We'll spend the rest of our lives together. And most of all, stuck in a place like Xinjiang, only your own family can mean something to you. Isn't that so?"

As he was babbling all this, his eyes seemed to blaze with indignation. I was somehow overwhelmed by his eloquence. I had nothing to say in reply, not a single word. The young soldier tried to calm the salesman, "Come on. He's only concerned about you. The girl is going with you and will be yours.

But this hasn't been decided yet, has it? We didn't know either of you. We poked our noses in it just because the girl is really pitiful. If you're reasonable, you'll see what we said is for the good of both of you. Don't you see it?"

The salesman nodded reluctantly. He seemed a little annoyed and angry, as though we'd done him some injustice. The others all tried to pacify him. Finally, he stood up, "In that case, I'll have to thank you people. But what do you think I should do now?" He looked at me again.

I asked the girl, "Are you sure it's all right for you?" The girl, all through this, hadn't even lifted her head. Now she nodded slightly and then returned to her silent pose.

The salesman said her, "If you agree, then we'd better move. I've got to buy you a ticket. If I'm too late, they'll be sold out."

The girl, without raising her head, whispered to me, "I'll never forget you," and walked away with the salesman.

Her simple words tugged at my heart. An idea suddenly occurred to me. I took out a piece of paper and wrote my name and address on it. I hurried to catch her and tell her to write me if in trouble. She cried when I gave her my address.

I stood there and watched them going. There was a distance between them, about a meter. In that gap I could see the railway station entrance. Two people of such different character and experience joined together like this. I noticed she maintained that distance from him, either from the natural modesty of a young girl or from some other reason. I had no way to find out. I watched them disappear in the crowd. My heart ached.

I never received a single word from the girl afterward. I guessed she must be living somewhere in distant Xinjiang. Maybe she was busy with housework; maybe she had had children. I only hoped the salesman was decent to her and gave her a bit of warmth and love in that difficult time. I didn't know why, but her figure often appeared before my eyes. I felt a little worried and restless. And perhaps, a bit guilty too.

In the fall of 1975, I went to Beijing on business. I suddenly found myself thinking about the girl. I was anxious to know about her situation. I found the address the salesman had given me. Oddly enough, there was no such place as No. 117. I thought I had probably gotten it wrong. I checked No. 17 and 77. Neither of them was right. I finally found the neighborhood committee and talked to an old lady representative. She told me there never had been such a family or anyone who went to Xinjiang from this place. No such person. I asked more questions but she started to get suspicious and began to question me about my name and identity. Why was I looking for such a person? She insisted on looking at my work card. Even then class struggle was still in full swing. Anybody could be a class enemy. If I kept on asking questions, next thing you know I'd find myself in the hands of the Public Security Bureau. So I left.

By then I realized I must have been duped by the so-called Xinjiang salesman. The girl was duped too. I was very angry. Maybe the girl was sold or suffered a worse fate. Perhaps she was no longer alive. I started to bitterly regret my actions. If I'd discouraged her, the girl might have had to go back to her brigade, but that wouldn't have been worse than being at the mercy of the salesman. It was entirely my fault. When she entrusted her future to me, I treated it far too casually. After all, it wasn't simply like a person asking you for directions. But if I hadn't done what I did, what else could I have done? No, that's only a rationalization. Ahh, I've never been much use to anybody. I guess I'm not much of a man. Whenever I think of this, I'll feel guilty about it.

I'll stop here. . . .

Now, I only hope I can find out where the girl is.

There is a picture I drew, a muddy road that merges into the sunlight in the distance.

I did it for the girl. I wish someday I could give it to her. Well, it's also a way for me to comfort my soul.

🙰

"In those days, the fate of one person was often the fate of millions."—F. J.

FOOTNOTE

1. Landlords, rich peasants, counterrevolutionaries, and "bad elements."

T W O

W I T N E S S E S

T O   A N

E X E C U T I O N

For subject:

T I M E: *1968* 🐦 A G E: *8 years old* 🐦 S E X: *Female*
P L A C E: *Y province, G city*

For narrator:

T I M E: *1979* 🐦 A G E: *37* 🐦 S E X: *Male*
O C C U P A T I O N: *A writer in T city*

I know you want to hear oral accounts of what happened during the Cultural Revolution from people who had profound experiences at that time, but I'd like to give you a secondhand account. It was related to me by the person who was directly involved.

The protagonist of this story was an eight-year-old girl who became a forced witness to an execution. You don't believe it? Yes, really . . . eight years old, not eighteen! Facing the barrel of a gun, she wasn't driven to despair—she thought it was a game! Don't be impatient . . . I'm going to tell you the story right away, exactly as it happened.

The time was 1979, the place Kunming. The border clash in Yunnan Province was still not over. My mission was to go to the front lines to cover what was happening. Not long after I arrived from Beijing, I suddenly had difficulty breathing. Someone told me that this was due to the high altitude of the plateau we were on and that as we moved further south, where the altitude would drop, I would feel better. So, not bothering to stay in Kunming even a day, I persuaded two friends who had accompanied me from Beijing, both painters, to take a jeep from Kunming to G city by way of K city. Once we reached G city we were told that if we wanted to continue south, we would have to hitch a ride with a military truck, as we would be going through the mountains where there would be no other means of transportation. But since it was already quite late when we arrived in G City, we knew that it would not be easy to hitch a ride, so we decided to spend the night in G City. The city itself seemed to have caught the war fever, with the streets full of soldiers as well as big trucks carrying munitions and other supplies. These trucks were covered with netting, underneath which were pine branches; in case of an air attack, the branches would act as camouflage. Also, the topic of discussion everywhere was the war. We tried to find lodgings in several hotels but didn't succeed because they were full. Finally, however, thanks to the good graces of the municipal committee, we found lodgings for the night in their guesthouse.

While we were eating dinner that evening in the guesthouse canteen, I was impressed with the industriousness of the waitress, a girl of about seventeen or eighteen years old. When she served us, however, she smiled. A pretty girl to begin with, she seemed even more so when she smiled. What was attractive about her wasn't the slick, "dolled-up" feminine beauty found in the cities, but the quality associated with the natural loveliness of Yunnan's mountains and lakes, something clear, luminous, unadorned. I have rarely seen such a pair of bright, shining eyes. When she opened those eyes of hers wide and looked at you, it was as if a high note on a grand piano had been struck. And when she smiled, you felt a rare kind of rapture.

She was not as short as the young women of Yunnan tend to be, and had the ruddy, simple features of a young woman from Northern China. When she came over with the dishes we had ordered, her arms bulged, her wrists were thick, and her fingers were plump, further proof of her northern extraction. Her beauty was inextricably wound up with her simple unsophisticated manners and bearing.

Intrigued by her demeanor, I ventured to ask her, "Why have you been smiling at me?" to which she responded, again beaming, "Because you're so tall." She spoke with a disarming honesty. Perhaps it was because I had become jaded by the pert loquaciousness of young women from the city, who knew so well how to put on airs and play games, that when I met someone as simple and honest as the young waitress in this restaurant, it was like leaving the city for the country, where—lo and behold—there were trees, pastures, birds, and trickling brooks. Her exceptionally unadulterated quality left me exhilarated.

My two traveling companions from Beijing were more attuned to beauty. Both were painters and, as you know, painters are by nature irresistibly drawn to beauty. So it was not surprising that the two of them asked her to come up to our room after she got off work so they could paint her portrait. But the young waitress's response to their invitation was uneasy until the two painters told her that I was a writer, at which point she looked at me without smiling and, without the least hesitation, nodded her head.

That evening she clearly came right after work, for she was still wearing her white work apron. As she entered our room, she dried her hands, which she had just washed and which were still dripping wet, on her apron. (Those small plump hands were bright red due to the cold water she had used to wash them.) The two painters asked her to sit down and then began to prop up their drawing boards. It was at this point that the young girl began to look a bit nervous. One of the painters whispered to me, "Talk to her . . . so that she'll relax."

Smiling, I then said to her, "Aren't you afraid of writers?"

To my surprise, she stated solemnly, "I was just looking for someone to write about me."

Laughing, I told her, "What's there to write about a young girl like yourself? Your runny nose when you cry?"

To my even greater astonishment, those radiant eyes of hers suddenly looked downcast. It was as if dark clouds had in an instant cast a shroud over the surface of a lake. A look of despair, anxiety, and suffering flooded those eyes. This was certainly not the look that a simple girl should have—it was instead the look of someone who suffered intensely.

As if speaking to herself, she murmured, "Okay, don't write it! I'll try to practice writing in the future—and then I'll write it myself!"

Stunned, I thought to myself, "Is it possible that this girl really has an unusual story to tell?" Convinced, that I should at least listen, I nodded my head and said to her, "Okay, start talking, and I'll write it down for you." And I never would have believed that she would tell me the following extraordinary tale.

"I was labeled a counterrevolutionary for ten years. It was

only last year that I was rehabilitated. My father was a midlevel cadre working for the municipal committee organization. We lived in one of the residential courtyards belonging to the municipal committee. At the beginning of the Cultural Revolution, I was only six years old, too young to really understand what was going on around me. So my memory of what happened during that time is fuzzy; I may have even mixed up some details. For instance, I remember that once a group of people stormed into our house and began to go through everything, turning our home upside down. As I recall, they boxed my ears, which needless to say was extremely painful. Later, my father said that no one had beaten me and that it was he alone who had been given a beating. What I remembered was probably just the feeling I experienced when I saw my father being beaten. Seeing him in pain had subconsciously aroused not only great mental anguish but also a kind of powerful physical sensation of pain as well. Before the Cultural Revolution began, my father had been the section chief of a department in charge of cadre affairs. Right from the beginning of the Cultural Revolution, he came under heavy attack and as a result fell from power. Later, the insurgents in my father's work unit—responding to Chairman Mao's call to ferret out counterrevolutionaries—split into two camps, one of which my father joined. But not long after this, the military—which was left-leaning—stepped in to support the other faction, which eventually spelled disaster for my father.

"Most of the people in my father's faction were midlevel cadres working for the municipal committee government, so their sense of discipline and responsibility was strong. As the Cultural Revolution had already rocked the lives of people high and low, these midlevel cadres were all the more afraid to engage in wanton acts of destruction—looting, smashing things, assaulting people, and so on—acts that would have left them open to attack by the other side. As a result, the other side found it very difficult to find a way to crush the faction my father was in. But one time when the two sides were in the middle of negotiating a truce, some of the members of my father's faction, without realizing it, were sitting on copies of the political journal *Red Flag*. Their opponents were on their toes and grabbed the copies out from under them. Flipping through the journals, they found photographs of Chairman Mao. Now at that time almost any issue of any magazine had a picture or photograph of the Chairman. So here was decisive evidence incriminating my father's side: insulting the honor of Chairman Mao—an unspeakable crime! 'Caught in the act!' The propaganda team of the People's Liberation Army immediately publicly announced that the faction my father belonged to was a counterrevolutionary organization. And this pronouncement resulted in my father's faction crumbling, beginning with the seizure of so-called enemies. Those who had run into trouble of a political kind in the past were labeled reactionary gangs, counterrevolutionaries, and 'revenge-bent' class enemies. Still, the other faction could not find a way to nail my father, because he simply did not have anything that bad in his record or background. But while my father had been chief of a cadre affairs department, he had offended a few people, who hated him as a result. They couldn't wait to grab the opportunity to bring him down, so they found a way to instigate an investigation of my father. But the longer they looked, the more frustrated and furious they became, because there simply were no skeletons in his closet.

"Even so, being investigated put a lot of pressure on my father. Although he had never been a cigarette smoker, he began to smoke heavily at this time. Once, while he was smoking in bed, he accidentally fell asleep. Although the cigarette burnt a big hole in the cotton mattress pad, thanks to my mother, who threw a basin of water and put the near fire out, my father was not hurt. If there really had been a fire, people would have said that he had been wantonly destroying things or else that he had been trying to commit suicide in order to avoid being prosecuted. The pressure on my mother was enormous, too. As she had a history of coronary trouble, the things that were happening made her condition worse—her heart would flutter and skip, causing her great physical pain. My whole family felt a great deal of anxiety, never knowing what terrible thing might happen next. Then one day something really unexpected did occur, and this time all eyes turned toward me.

"That day, graffiti appeared on one of the walls of the building complex we lived in. It said, 'Down with Chairman Mao!' The neighborhood committee alerted the local Public Security Bureau, which came and conducted an investigation. They concluded that the person who wrote the slogan must have been a child about 1.2 meters tall. This conclusion was based on the following alleged 'facts': First, the slogan had been written about a meter from the ground, which would have been too low for a grown-up standing up and too high for a grown-up squatting down to have written. The characters were at just the height that would have made it easy for a standing child to write them. Secondly, the characters were written in a childish scrawl. Third, an adult writing such a counterrevolutionary slogan would have given the person's entire name, in other words, would have written 'Down with Mao Zedong,' instead of 'Down with Chairman Mao.' Now in the residential quarters of the local municipal committee government, there were only eleven children whose height was 1.2 meters. These eleven were called together and forced to line up, and four likely suspects were chosen. The four 'chief suspects' were, as it turned out, the children of parents who had been in trouble in the past. In fact, it was naturally assumed that only the children of parents who had had 'problems' would dare write such slogans.

"Not long after this, the opponents of my father's faction intervened, saying they wanted to help the local Public Security Bureau to crack the case. Among themselves, though, they had already put me at the top of the list of suspects, citing as corroboration that my father was a reactionary and a sneaky underhanded type. They also firmly stated that he would do anything to vilify the Cultural Revolution, even egging me, his daughter, on to write such graffiti. (Of course, their real reason for going after me was still to clobber my father.) At that time, I was only eight years old.

"They called me over and began to offer me candy in hopes of getting me to talk. But ever since I was old enough to understand, my father had always made me tell the truth no matter what. Thus, it may have been because of my strict family upbringing that my father, in the end, was able to save himself.

"I refused to tell them what they wanted to hear, even after they had given me books and pictures, and even taken me to see movies. This made them furious, and a group of them one day surrounded me and began to pound the table, hit stools, and shout in my face—all in an effort to intimidate me. Furthermore, they told me that if I didn't tell them 'the truth' they would beat my father. Then they went into detail about how they would do it—for example, by using a fountain pen to poke out his eyes, using rope to string him up by the neck, starving him to death, and using a knife to carve him up, cutting off his fingers, ears, nose, and tongue and taking them piece by piece to the zoo to throw to the tigers. They even picked up a knife and pretended that they were going immediately to do the things they had threatened to do.

"In anguish and fear, I burst into tears, begging them not to, screaming ... but I didn't tell them any lies, even though, since I was only eight years old at the time, I was easily duped and frightened into submission. So why did I grit my teeth and refuse to go along with them? To tell the truth, I'm not sure myself. Now, thinking back on what happened scares me. What if I had fallen into their trap? One lie and my father would have been shot to death for sure in no time at all ... and I would not be here today either, because once I grew old enough to understand what had happened, I would have been so full of remorse and self-hate I would have killed myself.

"The intimidation did not stop there. In order to turn the screws even tighter, they labeled me a 'counterrevolutionary' and genuine criminal and had me locked up, not allowing me to see my parents at anytime. Although they didn't beat me, they often made me go hungry, and they would constantly interrogate me.

"But after a while, when these tactics didn't work and when they couldn't think of any other way to get me to confess, they had me taken to the headquarters of the municipal committee government, where I underwent struggle sessions. A wooden tablet was strung from my neck and I was also forced to wear a dunce cap. Both the tablet and the hat had the characters for 'active counterrevolutionary' and my name written on them. My name was crossed out with x's.

"I can't tell what took place with a great deal of precision because mentally I was in a state of confusion. I do remember a cacophony of human voices surrounding me, all shouts and slogans. My eyes were wide open but filled with tears, and my hair was disheveled. At one point, I screamed out, 'Ma! Ma!...' and then fainted. Later, after I had been released, my mother told me that she herself had not been there—even though she had been told that she had to go and watch my struggle session—because she had had some sudden heart trouble.

"One day—I can't tell you the exact date—but one that I will remember all my life...as soon as I began to talk about that day, I burst into...I can't help it...I'm sorry, I can't help it...OK, I'll tell you what happened.

"That day, they told me that they were going to execute me in front of a firing squad. I didn't know what 'execute in front of a firing squad' meant, so I asked them. They told me that it would be like in the movies, when the enemy is beaten at the end and taken out and shot to death. Hearing this, I began to cry. Would I ever see my mother and father again? I asked. They answered 'never' and added that I would never again play with my friends, see the world around me, or eat my favorite things. But, they said, if I confessed that it was my father who had made me write that counterrevolutionary slogan, they would not execute me. Shaking my head, I said over and over again, 'It wasn't me who wrote it. I want to see my mom and dad...'

"Then I was taken with a group of criminals who were also about to be executed to an execution ground, a large piece of low-lying ground.

"We were lined up in front of a large dirt pit. Everyone was tied up except for me. Even though I wasn't bound, I was dumbstruck with fear. Opposite us was a line of men pointing guns at us; there was one gun pointed directly at my face. Suddenly I saw my father quite nearby in a small crowd of people. (Later, I learned that they had forced my father to go there, and that he had to confess to having coaxed me into writing that graffiti or else ...) I started to call out to him—how I wanted to run over to him! But just at this moment, the officer in charge of the execution gave the order, 'Now!'

" 'Bang!' The bullets flew through the air and the row of prisoners all crashed to the ground, like a cabinet that had been tipped over and hits the floor. One brain flew through the air like a blood-filled egg. I was in such a state of terror that I didn't budge even a fraction of an inch, believing that I myself had been shot to death. But it was as if I didn't know I had been shot: I blinked a few times and twitched the corners of my mouth, as if to determine whether I was really alive or not. Meanwhile, my father had come running over to me and grabbed me. In an instant, he was hugging me tight. I asked him, 'Am I dead?' He answered, 'No, child ... don't be scared. They're teasing you. Those men didn't really die.' Hearing this, I let out a sigh of relief mixed with laughter and buried my head in Father's chest. I really believed that what had just taken place had been a game designed to frighten me and amuse my tormentors.

"Not long after, my father took me home to the comforting warmth of my family. I thought to myself, at last, everything is over. I ran over to play with my friends as I had done before. But strangely enough, none of them paid any attention to me; some of them even taunted and threw rocks at me. Once, one of my former best friends scolded me, saying, 'Down with the little stinking counterrevolutionary!' to my face. Furious at the insult, I chased him back to his house, trying to get him to apologize to me. But then his mother came out and began to yell at me, saying, 'What are you doing? Trying to reverse the verdict?'

"It was from this time on that, in a sense, I all of a sudden grew up, while I lost the ground from under my feet. This label of 'counterrevolutionary' was like a heavy boulder that I had to carry on my back for ten years. Going to elementary school was a trial and middle school was not any easier, for during those years, for instance, I was rejected out of hand by the junior and senior Red Guard organizations.

"It was as if I belonged to that class of unspeakably evil monsters made up of capitalist-roaders, class enemies, 'bad elements,' and so on, that at the time were under heavy fire and were social outcasts. So I didn't dare open my mouth except when it was absolutely necessary, or joke or play with my classmates. No matter how unreasonably or unjustly I was treated I never said a word of protest. Instead, every day after school was over, I would try to ingratiate myself with my classmates by sweeping the floor, wiping the blackboard, and straightening up the classroom. I would have been grateful for even the slightest look of human interest . . . in me . . . But during those eight years of school, I did not have a single good friend. I was a 'leper,' someone that people made a great effort to avoid. While I was in middle school I changed to a school that was farther away, believing that in this way my past might be forgotten as far as school was concerned. But even there, it was not possible . . . once when my class was sent out to the country to do manual labor, the political instructor assigned me to go and push the manure cart. No one else but me was given that job, something that I noted with astonishment. Without waiting for me to ask him why, the political instructor said to me, 'Manure may stink, but what you have inside you stinks even more.' It was then that I realized that I was still carrying that boulder on my back and that I would be doing it for the rest of my life. That night, I ran away, dashing off as fast as my legs would carry me. For two days and two nights I walked far out into the open country. My father eventually found me on the banks of a river waiting to die. Searching for me, my father had walked for two days, wearing out his shoes. Looking at him, I asked him, 'Why didn't they shoot me that time? Every day now for me is like being taken to the execution ground. . . .'

"Soon after returning home with my father, I dropped out of school and stayed at home to help my mother with household chores. With the exception of shopping for vegetables, I almost never ventured out of the house. I paid no attention to anyone, for life had expelled me to the very edges of a marginal existence. What interest could life have for me? In fact, there was no end to the daily boredom and listlessness that had become my life.

"With the fall of the Gang of Four, however, things took a sudden turn: When my father's work unit began to clear the debris from the cases left over from the Cultural Revolution, they discovered some documentation related to mine. This, they said, was sufficient to clear me and have me rehabilitated. But by then I was already nineteen years old, without a job, salary, housing . . . and my private belongings had been confiscated years ago. What good would 'rehabilitation' do me? Politics never takes responsibility for the souls of people.

"Nonetheless, the man in actual charge of my rehabilitation was not a bad person; in fact, he sympathized with me because of all that I'd been through. This, in turn, led him to think of a way to alleviate my troubles. It was, in fact, the only thing within his powers to do to help me. 'You're no longer a child, so it makes no sense to stay at home all the time—you should have a job. Why don't you go to the cafeteria of the municipal committee guesthouse and work there as a waitress?' he said to me.

"Hearing this, I thought to myself, 'However you look at it, my staying at home is a burden on my mother, who worries about my future but is too afraid to bring up the subject with me.' So I accepted the job, which I've been doing for only three months so far. In these months, though, I've worked harder than anyone else here. The others think I'm doing so much work out of a sense of gratitude for having been rehabilitated. Actually, that isn't the reason at all. How can I explain it to you?... Sometimes, I have a sudden flashback, and I see myself back in that classroom after school sweeping the floor—it's uncanny how at such times the feeling of guilt, of having committed a crime, gnaws away at me. It seems I can never break entirely free of it. Working in the cafeteria is like being in a labor reform camp—not a very pleasant experience at all. It's probably very difficult for you to imagine how I feel inside. At a very early age, I had to lower my head ... it is not easy now to raise it."

When she finished these words, it was as if something became caught in her throat. Nonetheless, there were neither tears in her eyes, nor a trace of emotion in her face, which was as calm as the sky on a day when the clouds have filled it completely with a dense, opaque white mass. Somewhere hidden behind those clouds, though, was, it seemed, the imminent possibility of thunder. But at the same time, I understood that those clouds would never again break into a downpour of rain and thunder. Despite her age, she had already gone through some of the most trying experiences that life can mete out to a human being. Turning to my two companions, I suddenly discovered that the two painters had been listening to her story with their mouths open and their eyes wide. There was nothing they could say, as there was nothing on their sketch pads, not even the beginnings of a drawing. The blank paper that lay there was like the feeling that I felt myself deep within—an emptiness that was frightening.

The victims of true cruelty are always the innocent.—F. J.

THE PAPER COLLECTOR WANTS TO SAVE HER HUSBAND

For subject:
TIME: *1968* ❧ AGE: *31* ❧ SEX: *Male*
OCCUPATION: *Language teacher in a commune primary school in S province*

For narrator:
TIME: *1972* ❧ AGE: *35* ❧ SEX: *Male*
OCCUPATION: *Cadre in the propaganda section of a tank division in S province, I city*

At that time, I was a cadre in the propaganda section of a tank division in ... province. In 1973, we received an order from higher authorities to go to the southwestern part of Shandong Province to give support to the Leftist struggle there. The social turbulence created by the Cultural Revolution had subsided, relatively speaking, and violence erupted only sporadically. In fact, the great tidal wave that had carried the country through such great spasms had run its course. Most of our work involved clearing up the disorder that had been created in the past five years.

The county that we were sent to was near Liangshan, the

setting for the Ming dynasty novel *The Water Margin*. We were staying at a hostel run by the county authorities that, according to legend, was the Black Dragon residence of Song Jiang, the novel's bandit hero. Nearby was a fairly ramshackle pagoda that also dated from the same era as the events described in *The Water Margin*. There were 108 of us all together, exactly the same as the number of renegades in Song Jiang's band. We all had a good laugh, saying to ourselves, "The 108 plucky bandits have returned to Liangshan!" And, really, who wouldn't have wanted to go and see the setting for the most famous of Chinese novels? So naturally, we were in good spirits when we started out.

But we hadn't expected that the sparse, barren setting that was the base for the novel's renegade heroes would remain unchanged eight hundred years later. The area bordered the Yellow River, and so the soil was characteristically of the saline-alkaline type found in the lower reaches of that river. The year before, the flooding of the river had left deposits of silt and sludge that had dried up the following spring, leaving the earth spattered with large, packed clods of sludge. The spring was so dry that the buds of the willows withered and died before they had a chance to become leaves. How desolate the area was!

The topography was nothing like the way it was described in *The Water Margin*. Instead of towering mountains, there was a series of small hills. But the people of the county looked as if they had just stepped out of the novel: They wore buttonless garments with large, crossed lapels, a belt pulled tight at the waist, and a pocket in front where they could carry a hunk of meat or a bottle of wine. They sat anywhere, eating dog meat, drinking heartily, and displaying an earthy kind of boorishness.

We were living at that time in the county seat. As a military representative, I became a member of the standing committee of the county revolutionary government. Although this was only a temporary stint, in the first few days after my arrival I was already deluged with a number of matters involving aggrieved parties seeking redress. Some of these cases bordered on the astounding—some of them could have been included in a sequel to that book *Ancient and Modern Miracles*.

One day while I was in my dormitory room, an extremely thin man wearing a pair of round spectacles came into my room, bent down to the floor, and began to grovel at my feet. When I asked him what the matter was, he answered: "If you are really willing to help me solve my problem, I will tell you. If you just want to get rid of me, then say so and I will go away ... in which case my coming here will have been in vain."

What a straight-talking, feisty man he was! I told him, "I treat all matters that come to my attention very carefully. There's no way I would try to keep you at arm's length."

"But the problem I have is a very difficult one."

"I'm not afraid of difficulty, just as long as you tell me the truth."

Fixing on me his intense gray eyes, he sat down on a bench and began telling me a most unusual story.

The man's name was Li. He lived about thirty-five kilometers from the county seat next to the ancestral home of Pan Jinlian, the heroine of the famous erotic novel, *The Golden Lotus*. There he taught Chinese in a commune elementary school. Li was a gifted storyteller. He could remember all the stories that had been told to him as well as the ones he himself had read in books. It was as if he simply stored them up in his belly, and when need be, all he had to do was open his mouth and the stories would come gushing out. What was even more remarkable was that he would rarely tell the same story twice to the same audience. He was the kind of teacher who could extemporaneously and effortlessly give a lesson to his students. His talk was filled with humor, lively anecdotes, and human interest, which must have made his classes extremely popular with the students, who seemed reluctant to leave when the bell rang at the end of class. That in itself says something, as everyone knows that elementary school children love to hear the bell ring so they can scamper out and play during recess.

One of the forerunners of the Cultural Revolution was the Socialist Education Movement of 1965. It was characterized, in part, by whole-hearted zeal to express loyalty and devotion to Chairman Mao, which translated into turning over desks and cabinets, rummaging through chests, and so forth, all in order to ferret out persons or actions deemed disloyal to the Chairman. During the "Antirightist" campaigns, every work unit would set out to round up "right-leaning elements" according to quotas fixed by the higher authorities. Thus, each work unit would have to come up with a certain number of "rightist elements" and whenever an antirightist movement was launched, not being able to "come up with the numbers" was a sign of failure on the part of a work unit. Things reached the point where the more a work unit surpassed its quotas, the brighter its achievements shone.

Li's school was a case in point. It seemed as if the whole place rose up to rummage through the past so as to come up with missteps, crimes, suspicious actions, and whatnot in order to pin the label "Rightist" on others.

With his rather prickly personality, Li had offended a few of his colleagues, and one of them declared that he had once heard Li tell a story about how Chairman Mao had once had to jump into a ditch and lie down in it to avoid being captured by the White Army, which was hot on his heels. Such an account, it was charged, was an obvious attempt to smear the Chairman. How could the Great Leader allow the enemy to make him jump into a ditch in the fields and then lie down in it? What an intentional effort to distort the Chairman's image! The leaders of the school immediately went through all the pupils' books and papers and, in the end, found one of the students' language textbooks, in the margin of which was written: "A story about how Chairman Mao, using his wits, hid himself in a ditch to escape from the enemy's clutches." Here was irrefutable evidence! So a report charging Li with having engaged in very serious counterrevolutionary activities was sent up to the county committee. Soon afterward, the Public Security Bureau apprehended him. But Li refused to admit to any wrongdoing. Defending himself, he said, "I told this story to show how clever and brave Chairman Mao was. Also, this story wasn't my own —I got it out of a book." But when the Public Security Bureau asked him in which book he had read it, he couldn't remember, try as he might. Without such evidence, the facts still pointed to Li's guilt. Furthermore, it seemed to the Public Security Bureau that Li was only trying to cover up his guilt by spinning still another story about the existence of such a book, which only showed how devious and stubborn he was! The verdict came down swiftly and succinctly: eight years' imprisonment.

Li's wife was a woman from the country. They had only been married a little over a year when this unfortunate turn of events occurred. Six months pregnant, she went to pay her husband a visit in prison. He told her, "Eight years in prison is a long time. If you can't endure such a long separation, you can get a divorce; I won't blame you if you do. And I'm really telling you the truth; I really did read that story in a book. . . ." After her visit Li's wife ran over to the county committee headquarters to protest that her husband had been wronged. The county leaders told her, "Go and find some proof. Once you have, we'll release your husband."

Being a simple country woman, Li's wife really believed that all she had to do was produce such proof and her husband would be freed. So she went off every which way to search for it. At that time, the Cultural Revolution had just begun, and the bookstores in the county seat carried only the works of Chairman Mao. Also, the libraries were closed to show revolutionary spirit. Li's wife went and spoke to the man in charge of the local library to see if she could find the book in which her husband had found the incriminating story. But the librarian was scared of lifting the strips of paper saying BOARDED UP which were pasted to the doors. After all, if he did, wouldn't he be setting himself up to be attacked as "revisionist" or "capitalist"? Besides this librarian was the best-read person in the county and had never come across such a story about Mao.

Even though she had failed in this attempt, she continued her search wherever she went. If she couldn't find any books lying around, she would pick up other printed matter. But because she was illiterate, she had to prevail on relatives or even primary school children to read them aloud to her. Sometimes she would come upon a small leaflet or newsletter to do with the Cultural Revolution that had been printed only just recently, and would have it read to her. All her life she had lived in poverty in the countryside, so she had no cultural awareness. She didn't know how many books might exist altogether at that time. Nor did she have any idea what the characters of the written language might contain. When someone read her something about politics, science, or culture, she would be dumbfounded, not knowing what to make of the strange incomprehensible things that were being read to her, still waiting to hear that story about Chairman Mao's hiding himself in a ditch. . . . Finally, people began to get tired of having to read the bits of paper she brought them and would look them over in a cursory way and tell her, "The story's not there." Believing that the person had really tried, she would continue looking for other printed materials.

One day, someone tried to give her some advice, saying, "Do you really think you're going to come across your husband's story by picking through anything that has print on it? First of all, you can't read. Second, God knows how many pages of printed matter there are. How are you ever going to find, let alone read, all of them? Wise up!" But no one could reason with her. She continued to go through the streets every day carrying a shabby basket in which she collected scraps of paper. All she had to do was see something that had characters on it, and she would pounce on it as if it were some precious gem. And if she spied someone holding something printed, she would implore him or her to give it to her. If the person refused, Li's wife would ask him to tell her what was written on it. If this request were also turned down, she would go down on her knees and beg the person to read it to her. She even became so desperate that she would collect the bits of paper she found in the public toilets,[1] clean them, and then ask someone to read them to her! This cycle was repeated day in and day out: Collect scraps of paper, have them read out loud to her, and not find the story. The hope she felt at daybreak would disappear by nightfall. Nonetheless, she never became discouraged, always believing firmly that the story had not been her husband's invention. But as time went on, she couldn't help but become somewhat demented. She would carry her baby on her back while picking up paper. When the child was older, he would follow his mother on her paper-collecting rounds. The paper that she went through she eventually sold to make a living. For miles around Liangshan, people saw this half-crazed woman paper collector whose wide-open eyes had a lost, bleary stare. They saw her always leading her poor little child and carrying her decrepit straw basket full of paper, but they didn't necessarily know that she was not scrounging around for paper to eke out a living. Nor did they know that the real reason was that a gleam of hope that she might yet save her husband still flickered in her.

All year round—spring, summer, autumn, and winter—in snow, ice, wind, and cold, she carried on her search, never stopping for so much as a day. But such earnest devotion could not necessarily move heaven to intercede on her husband's behalf. She collected paper unremittingly for over seven years. Then one day, six months before her husband's prison sentence was up, her stove accidentally set fire to the pile of paper that had accumulated in the corner of her house. In the conflagration that followed, she and her child both lost their lives.

When Li heard the news of their deaths, he lost all desire to go on living. He tried several times to commit suicide, but without success. He failed because the prison was practically bare. The county jail he was imprisoned in was singularly lacking in any and all material trappings for two reasons: First, it was badly off financially, and second, the jailers feared that the inmates might commit suicide if they had the material means to. For instance, after a meal, the bowls were taken away immediately to prevent the prisoners from taking them and later smashing them into shards and cutting their own wrists.

One time, when Li went to use the toilet, he saw a piece of rope hanging from the ceiling of the outhouse. He took it and tied it to one of the roof beams. Then, using both hands, he grabbed hold of the roof beam and pulled himself high enough so he could slip the noose he had made around his neck. Just as he took his hands away to hang himself, the rope broke and he fell face-first—splat!—to the ground. He saw stars, golden ones.

But just as he was recovering from this kinesthetic kaleido-scope, a miracle happened: A mimeographed piece of paper appeared before him on the ground. And there was the story that had been the scourge of his life—he couldn't believe his own eyes! As the Chinese proverb goes, "Heaven finds a way to help a man before all is lost." You don't believe it? It really happened! On that ragged scrap of paper was that story, still partially intact. Part of it went as follows: "The man began to chase after him again . . . he started to shout, 'He's escaped!' and began to chase after Mao Zedong. . . . But by this time, Mao was going down the other side of the hill." Although only part of the story was there, it would still show that it was the work of someone other than Li. So, taking the scrap of paper, Li rushed out of the outhouse and began to yell, "I've found it! I've got the evidence that will clear me!" He was so exhilarated by the discovery that in his excitement he began to jump up and down. The jailer who saw him thought he must surely be mad and so locked him up in one of the cells. No matter, though; holding the piece of paper in his hands, Li continued to laugh wildly. But the laughter turned into a gale of sobbing, as Li started to form images in his mind of the eight years his poor wife had spent picking up paper. . . . But she hadn't been able to make it through to today! And what about his poor little son?

Without delay, Li wrote an appeal and sent it, along with the scrap of paper containing the story, to the county authorities. All he had to do now, he thought to himself, was to wait for the wrong that had been done him to be righted and then he would be out of jail! But several days later, the county authori-ties declared that the scrap of paper had been mimeographed and that therefore it was inadequate proof—after all, who knows where it had been printed or who had written it and when? So Li's appeal was summarily turned down.

Nonetheless, Li did not despair—in fact, he was more sure than ever that he would be vindicated. With that scrap of paper, he would sooner or later find the whole story intact. At one time in the past, while in prison, Li had actually suddenly been seized with fear that perhaps he really had not read the story somewhere, that perhaps instead he had heard it from some idle mouth, in which case it would be impossible ever to absolve himself. But now, at least, Li was not tortured by the nagging worry that he might not really have read the story.

The day Li came to talk with me, he had already served his eight-year prison term; his grievances had still not been redressed. Because he had served a sentence as a counterrevolutionary, the elementary school he had worked at before refused to allow him to continue working there. Without any income, much less the means to go to a larger place to look for the book in which the story had originally appeared, he was really in dire straits. All he had was the clothing on his back, which was hardly enough to keep out the spring cold. When he walked into my office, he was shivering.

After he had told me his story, I said to him, "Why don't you go now? I'll take care of this matter for you."

Getting such a brusque, to-the-point answer from me, Li appeared skeptical of my intentions, assuming that I was simply trying to get rid of him. But never in a hundred years would he have believed that I had read the very same story or that I knew the whereabouts of that book. I felt the blood rush to my temples as I thought about the power that was in my hands to release Li from the great burden that he had been carrying for over eight years.

The next day, I went to the headquarters of the county Party committee to look at the file on Li's case. At a specially convened meeting of the committee, I brought up the matter of Li's conviction. Some of the committee members sighed in exasperation, "What? That again? What is it about this man that makes him so tenacious? There's no way to stop him, is there?"

I said, "The law does not exist in order to correct personalities. There really was such a story published and the ruling was unjust. We've got to redress his grievance!"

As a military representative, I had greater authority than the others, who therefore sat there in silence, not daring to make a rebuttal. At this point, infuriated by their inability to take a stand, I ordered a car, went back to the army unit, brought back the book in which the story had appeared, and laid it on the desk for the members of the county Party committee to read.

The book? A volume of revolutionary memoirs, with a reddish-violet cover, published by the Liberation Army's Literary Publishing House. The title? *The Autumn Harvest Uprising and the Establishment of the People's Army.* Opening the book, I flipped to the story that had been at the root of all of Li's troubles: "A Narrow Escape From Danger in Liuyang" by a man named Xie Juezai. It recounted how once when Chairman Mao was traveling to the revolutionary base in Jiangxi Province he had been captured by the White Army, and how he had managed to throw them off by jumping into a ditch.

When the leaders of the committee looked at the book, they were so stunned that they couldn't speak. Only one of them ventured to say under his breath, "How could old Xie write such a thing!"

So it happened that due to a story he had retold eulogizing Mao Zedong, a mountain-village teacher had been charged with having "opposed" the Chairman and then been imprisoned for eight years, during which time his family, as well, had met with calamity and an untimely death. Is it possible that this was just an unfortunate twist of fate, a punishment meted out to mortals? I, for my part, was unwilling to let this case slip through my fingers. I watched it very closely to its very end, which came quickly. Through my own unstinting efforts, I was able to have Li rehabilitated. The day that this happened, Li ran over to my house, fell to his knees, and again began to grovel in front of me so demonstratively that you would have thought he was thanking his guardian angel.

While he was kowtowing before me, I was overcome with a feeling of apprehension and bewilderment: After all, I had only happened upon the case by chance . . . what right did I have to accept prostrate offerings of gratitude from the victim of such great suffering? I was silent for a long while, not knowing at all what to say, only occasionally murmuring, "Yes, yes, I know. . . ."

Before leaving, Li begged me to give him the book that had brought him such misfortune, and had, ironically, exonerated him in the end, too. So much of his life lay between its covers. . . . I agreed to his request, and Li took the book slowly into his trembling hands, as if it were an immense load entrusted to him. Afterward, I heard that he had burned the book and sprinkled the ashes on his wife's grave. I suppose he made a wish that the spirit of his poor country wife would henceforth be at peace.

After Li's case, the number of people who came with appeals multiplied manyfold. Every day, there would be people outside my door, their numbers great enough to block access to the inside. Still later, when I left the military and went back to my hometown in Anhui Province, the provincial party committee sent me to implement a new government policy. I did not expect such a tiny county seat to have so many aggrieved persons all appealing for redress of past injustices. These people would line up day and night just to see me. They were there from the time I went to my office until I went home. Furthermore, none of their cases were as straightforward to straighten out as Li's had been. They involved the broadest array of injustices and breaches of ethical conduct, some so bizarre as to make any attempt at remedy extremely difficult indeed. It would have been well nigh impossible to have gotten involved in many of them, and even if I had, I would have been dragged into situations which I would not have been able to extricate myself from. It was then that I realized that I alone could not possibly even begin to pick up the pieces of the gigantic tragedy that this era had created.

I was only able to sleep a few hours every night. The problems that I could resolve I dealt with. As for those that I could not tackle, I wrote up special reports about them and sent these to the provincial Party committee for further review.

From my own experience trying to resolve these matters, I can fairly state that the personal mishaps and tragedies that befall the great and well-known cannot compare with those that ordinary people go through. The injustices that happen to famous people are relatively easy to rectify, generally speaking. But ordinary people are up against much more difficult odds—and these odds depend on their meeting the right person or hitting on the right opportunity. Otherwise, the chances of their ever seeing a "clear patch of sky" in the otherwise gray fog of injustice that completely blankets their horizons is dim indeed. I wonder to myself: How many people living today have mental scars that have not healed or been attended to?

"The experiences of the people are the experiences of history."—F. J.

F O O T N O T E

1. Newspapers and other printed matter are sometimes used as toilet paper in China.

T H E

M O S T

I N T E L L I G E N T

M A N

TIME: *1969*   🦋 AGE: *15*   🦋 SEX: *Male*
OCCUPATION: *High school student in S province, S city*

Who didn't suffer during the Cultural Revolution? There were hundreds of millions of victims, each worse off than the other. Take, for example, my brother-in-law, a brilliant speaker who could out-debate anyone. He was caught in the cross fire and the other side tore out his tongue. Not only could he not speak, there was also no way he could eat, so in the end he starved to death. In some ways, that era could be compared to the great Tangshan earthquake of 1976. There were both victims and survivors. The Cultural Revolution was the great earthquake brought about by Chairman Mao, while the Tangshan earthquake was the revolution set in motion by the gods of the land. But let's not dwell on those tragic details any longer. I'll tell you a story with a slightly different twist, OK? I'd like to talk to you about a really extraordinary incident and an extraordinarily intelligent man. Although everyone says that during the Cultural Revolution, people's talents and wisdom were stifled, this wasn't universally true. In the midst of all the danger, there were some who managed, while playing with fire, to display their acumen and their ability. The man I just referred to was able to do this. He wasn't someone I had only heard of but someone I met personally.

Wasn't 1969 a year when China was making special efforts to be prepared in case of war and natural disasters? Everyone was considered a soldier fighting for this great worthy cause. So as soon as Chairman Mao had issued the order, the whole country threw itself into field training. Besides schools and the civil bureaucracy, even factories and stores began to organize themselves in quasi-military fashion. Contingents of workers would go regularly into remote areas to undergo military training while marching long distances, sometimes several hundred kilometers. The farther they walked, the more they suffered, and thus the more "revolutionary" they were considered. I'm sure you went through such experiences! Wearing military uniform, carrying the red flag, these contingents crossed field and mountain, oblivious to hardship or reason... speaking of which, I must tell you that everyone, yes, everyone, had gone mad. We all wondered where the enemy was lurking or where the evil powers blew from. It was rather like small children playing a game of "pretend," with the false being taken for granted as true.

At that time, I was in high school. The day we began our field training, everyone in my contingent was boiling with excitement. Wearing our jungle-green uniforms as well as army shoes and caps—some of my classmates had even gotten five-gold-star insignia from their relatives or friends in the military and pinned them to the front of their caps—we really were the spitting image of fresh new army recruits. The girls had piled their hair inside their caps and were wearing leather belts around their waists and had slipped green canvas bags diagonally over their shoulders. On these canvas bags were embroidered the five characters meaning "serve the people." Inside were copies of the *Quotations of Mao Zedong* as well as food rations. Those were the days when people had character—all they needed were the *Quotations of Mao Zedong* and sufficient food rations, and they were fine. It wasn't at all like today, when everyone feels they can't live without a color TV, refrigerator, washing machine, and tape recorder. And that's right, before I forget it, pinned to everyone's chest was a badge with Chairman Mao's likeness on it. The badge I was wearing was one that I had dug down deep into my drawers to find. It was the nicest badge I had. The kind of badges we were wearing at the time were called, in the jargon of those in the know, "the eighty-round steamships." "Eighty-round" referred to the fact that the diameter of these badges was eighty millimeters, about the size of a *shao bing*.[1] These "eighty-round" badges were the largest available. The size of these badges mattered in that the larger they were, the more loyal the wearer supposedly was— and certainly the more startlingly visible they were. The "steamship" referred to a steamship tossing in a windswept, stormy sea, whose helmsman, of course, was Chairman Mao, without whom the ship would be lost. On these badges, the image of the Chairman and the ship itself were copperplate that shone with a luster like gold. Behind the ship, above the sea, was a large red sun. The badge itself was coated with a layer of the kind of bright paint found on the five-star badges that were pinned to caps at the time. All in all, these "eighty-round" badges were the newest, largest, and most fashionable of their kind at the time. There was not the slightest doubt that they were works of great craftsmanship. Stealing glances at the "eighty-round" badge pinned to my clothes, how my classmates envied me! Especially pleased with myself, believing myself to be the most loyal to the cause, I would walk proudly with my head held high, with more than a touch of exhibitionism.

One day, the school invited a company of the People's Liberation Army to take us on a round of field training. Spotting the company commander, I immediately felt respect for and took a liking to him. He was a man of about thirty, and there was something in his demeanor that set him apart from others. Maybe it was his erect posture, his height, or the carriage of a military officer which he so authoritatively possessed. His thin lips were usually tightly closed, so rarely did he ever seem to talk. Above them to the left was a black mole. Although he had a light complexion and handsome features, there was something stern about him. That mole of his never moved, a fact that never ceased to fascinate me. He really did seem to have stepped out of a movie—he had the cool, unruffled look of a matinee idol of the silver screen. Although my classmates and I were on very familiar terms with the soldiers in the company, we all kept our distance from him. None of us dared to speak to him. His last name was Bai.

The company command divided the soldiers into two groups and did the same with us, so that each group of soldiers led one group of students. Bai led one combined soldier-student group, and the political instructor the other. Each subcompany set out on a different route. Luckily, I was assigned to the subcompany that Bai was leading.

Our subcompany, in turn, was divided into three platoons, each led by a platoon leader who marched in front of the group. There was also one soldier in each platoon who carried a red flag. I was in the first platoon, the foremost of the three. Our platoon was led by a red flag carrier who was immediately followed by a tall soldier carrying a huge bust of Chairman Mao, the kind one most often saw at the time, made of white porcelain. While marching, we would shout slogans in unison, recite quotations of the Chairman's, and sing revolutionary songs. Thus, our heroic spirits filled the air of the open country lying before us. The light bouncing off the red flag and the flag itself seemed to be reflected in our faces. The feeling in the air was like what it must have been when the Red Army in the late 1920s began to move up north to fight as well. We felt our whole bodies fill up with energy.

Now, of course, in hindsight, it all seems ridiculous. What enemy were we talking about? In the fields, aside from birds, there were only field mice to be found. Nonetheless, from early morning until it grew dark outside, we didn't feel the least bit tired. But the platoon leader, fearing that the tall soldier carrying the porcelain bust of Chairman Mao was exhausted, began to look for someone to replace him. Immediately all the soldiers in the platoon jumped up and began to clamor, each vying for the privilege of carrying the bust. We students, too, all threw our hats into the ring, hoping to take on that honored responsibility, since everyone believed that whoever in the end successfully competed for the honor would be the most loyal to Chairman Mao among us.

But to everyone's disbelief, the tall soldier who had been carrying the porcelain bust refused to relinquish his responsibility, declaring in an agitated, booming voice, "I am going to protect Chairman Mao on the new Long March." This fellow originally was from Shandong Province, so he had the honest, plain looks characteristic of people from Shandong. His pledge filled me with admiration for him. His loyalty and sincerity made the "eighty-yuan" badge on my chest seem very ordinary and unworthy of attention.

As soon as he had finished his pledge, we students began to shout a slogan, "Let us study the example of the People's Liberation Army! Let us salute the People's Liberation Army!" And the soldiers answered at once in one grand voice, "Let us study the example of these young revolutionary generals! Swear to protect with our lives the Party and the Central Committee! Swear to protect with our lives Chairman Mao!" This exchange continued for several rounds, all the while increasing in emotion and volume. It seemed as if, by doing this, we could make our voices heard across the open country by others wherever they were, as well as crush the enemy, wherever he might be hiding.

But this burst of energy gradually dissipated as we continued marching even as it got pitch-black outside and we became engulfed in the night. By the wee hours of the morning, we were all quite tired. By this time, as well, our cries had tapered off without our being aware of it. In the still darkness, only our footsteps could be heard. Although the soldiers in our platoon were still marching in step, we students—not of very much use, to tell the truth—could barely stand up straight. Moreover, our empty stomachs began to grumble. Taking advantage of the darkness and the rustling of the branches and leaves of the forest we happened at one point to be walking through, we reached into our canvas shoulder bags and grabbed some steamed bread, which we stuffed into our mouths. Afraid of being seen, we hastily chewed and then swallowed the whole lump down. Not long after, Commander Bai, who was marching at the very back, dispatched an orderly to inform us that after crossing the next highland, we would be arriving in Baige Village, where we would take a rest. When the orderly told us this good news, how we wished we could reach that village in one bound, throw ourselves down on the ground, and fall asleep.

But since there was no shortcut, we had to make our way over the highlands, and even then we still couldn't see any sign of the village. In fact, up ahead it was still pitch-black, with not so much as a glimmer of lantern light. On the left was a river bright with the reflected light of the moon. The clamor of the water flowing was distinctly audible. On our right was a field of sorghum, whose stalks were blowing in the wind, making a rustling sound rather like falling rain. The field itself was a formidable sight—a seemingly infinite wall of shining blackness. The night mist seemed to have soaked into the ground, making our shoes swoosh as we walked. At the same time, our shoes increasingly began to stick to the ground, which made our feet seem even heavier. Our feet didn't seem to be our own: Instead, they had all the weight and inertness of two bricks. I couldn't even pluck up the courage to ask how much farther away the village was—after all, this was field training in preparation for a war that was going to be fought! If I had asked, it would have been inviting someone to attack me for thinking about such things, and that would lead to my being the object of group criticism. So we all continued marching ahead without mouths gagged. What a different sight we were compared to that afternoon! We were like an army that had just been defeated coming home.

Suddenly we heard someone at the front of our platoon let out a shout of startled fear. At the same time we heard a loud thud and then the sounds of something shattering—it sounded like the great porcelain bust of Chairman Mao had fallen to the ground and was flying into bits and pieces. Everyone looked around. And the worst had actually happened. The tall soldier who had been carrying the bust had slipped and the unthinkable had occurred: The great porcelain bust of the Chairman had fallen to the ground and broken. Think about it yourself: For a whole day that poor fellow had been carrying a porcelain bust of the Chairman that weighed over ten kilograms. How could he not have been completely exhausted? Indeed, if he'd had any strength left at all, he would have held on for dear life to that half-statue. He would have been willing to hurtle himself to the ground in order to cushion the figure from breaking. On the other hand, who asked him to hold onto the statue so obstinately when he was way past the point of total exhaustion? When the platoon leader had tried to get someone to replace him, he had refused to relinquish the bust. However, still too stunned to say anything, no one thought of blaming him. Breaking the icon of the Chairman was a dreadful crime of hideous proportions. Without waiting for us to wake up to what had happened, the tall fellow suddenly fell to the ground and, kneeling in front of the broken pieces of the bust, began to beg forgiveness! And the platoon leader, who had let such an appalling thing happen, involuntarily fell to the ground himself, begging pardon, too! Then the whole platoon, without waiting for the order, fell to its knees.

A short while afterward, the second platoon arrived on the scene. Seeing us all kneeling on the ground, they wondered what had happened. When the commander of the second platoon asked us what the meaning of all this was, no one dared to reply. A few people, however, pointed straight ahead, so the second platoon leader walked over and, seeing the shattered remains of the bust, fell to his knees at once without a single word.

This, in turn, set his own men to falling down on their knees in one great *swoosh*. When the third platoon arrived, led by Company Commander Bai, the latter knew at a glance what had taken place. Without waiting for him to say anything or to think what to do, the third platoon and its leader all fell to their knees like a row of frightened dominoes—everyone wanted to be the first to drop down, for that would mean that he was the most thoroughly loyal, the most resolute. But this platoon was like a bow that had been stretched too tight, so that when it came time to release it, everyone collapsed to the ground at the same time, including Company Commander Bai. But all this kneeling meant that there was a knotty problem to deal with: how to stand up again! Whoever got to his feet, by reverse logic, would be disloyal! Nonetheless, this kneeling could not go on indefinitely. On the other hand, who was to say when it should end? We would even have to kneel until dawn came; there was simply no way out. Under the moon and stars, the wilderness around us, like the dirt road we were kneeling on, was one black mass. Whether out of madness or out of stupidity, there in the midst of this black emptiness was a huge phalanx of men on their knees, not one of them daring to utter a sound, look at another person, or even twitch a muscle. Filled with a kind of remorse over the crime that had been committed, they looked straight ahead at that pile of shattered porcelain, which was gleaming white under the moonlight.

Kneeling . . . kneeling . . . gradually I began to be aware of a growing pain in my right knee. Using my hand to feel around, I discovered that my left calf had been right on top of a rock whose sharp edge was sticking out of the ground. After struggling a long time, I was able to use my fingers to dig it out of the ground and, without making a sound, I cast it to the side. Not much time had elapsed, though, before I had the sudden urge to urinate. The more uncomfortable I felt, the more I felt like urinating, but how on earth could I manage to do it? Even so, when things got to the point where I couldn't endure the pain any longer, I urinated. It was really—damn it—morally reprehensible. The crotch of my pants was dripping wet, so there I was in discomfort again.

Time began to slow down, moving second by second. The longer we knelt, the less reason there seemed to be to stand up. But then all of a sudden, Company Commander Bai in one fell swoop stood up, brushing the ground as he did. His usually clear, resonant voice had an anxious ring, as if he were under great stress or something had gone wrong.

"A bad turn of events! Something's astir up ahead in the village—it's the enemy! Perhaps the reactionary elements of the landlord class are engaged in sabotage right at this very moment! I want everyone—all three platoons—to assemble together so that we can move swiftly. Our objective is to reach Baige Village up ahead and protect the poor and lower middle-class peasants, the Great Proletarian Cultural Revolution, and the Party and Chairman Mao!"

This order—to protect the Chairman—was a task more important than that of protecting our own lives. The urgency of it made the several hundred of us still kneeling on the ground jump up at once. In that twinkling of an eye, I suddenly felt a kind of relief and at the same time a kind of nervousness. If the enemy was really up ahead, then wouldn't we be fighting a battle soon? In any case, our troops were on the ball: In no time, we had assembled into orderly ranks and under Commander Bai's direction were marching at a rapid pace straight ahead. With the enemy right in front of us, and the situation a tinderbox, who had time to think about that shattered porcelain bust? All we had to make sure of was that we didn't step on the pieces as we marched past them.

After a little more than ten minutes, we turned right, went over a bridge, and then hurried along for another ten minutes. A dog was barking in the distance up ahead, a vast, empty space shrouded in night mist. But through all this the light of a few lanterns could be seen. Thus, the village had to be straight ahead of us.

The villagers had originally gone to bed and extinguished their lamps. But with our impending arrival, one by one people woke up and lit their lanterns to see what the commotion was about. The village dogs, too, started to bark wildly. There was something tense and imminent in the air: Was there going to be a battle? Our hearts started to beat wildly, the blood in our veins began to pound. The soldiers took off the rifles that they had been carrying on their backs and, holding them in their hands, began running toward the village, as Commander Bai gave the order for each platoon to advance separately, with the students at the back.

As we entered the village, we made out the light of torches and some human figures, as well as the moving light from some flashlights directly in front of us. Although the human figures were somewhat indistinct, we could make out the rifles they were carrying. Were these human figures counterrevolutionaries bent on sabotage? Before we had any time to consider the answer to this question, Commander Bai yelled out to the crowd of figures carrying torches, "Don't open fire. We're PLA people on a round of field training. Who are you people? What is the situation now in the village?"

A man with a huge, bellowing voice yelled back from the other side, "We're the local militia. We heard a lot of shouting and dogs barking, and we didn't know what to make of it!"

"What about the 'four bad elements'?"

"They're all at home behaving themselves. They're not allowed to come out at night."

As his troops slowly moved toward where he was standing, Bai explained to the local militia, "We have been doing field training and just happened to pass by. Hearing some commotion, we sensed that something was amiss—and we suspected that the 'four elements' might be engaged in sabotage or insurrection! So we rushed over to lend you support. If there's no such danger, fine!"

The leader of the local militia now spoke. "Our thanks go to you, our beloved People's Liberation Army, for having worried about us poor and lower middle-class peasants. In our village, there's an empty elementary school building no longer being used because the school is in the throes of revolution. Please come in and rest yourselves. We'll go and get water and boil it so you can drink something..." On finishing these words of gratitude, he immediately called several of his people to go and fetch water, light stoves, and borrow some quilts and mattress pads.

So our company of men entered the schoolhouse to rest, drink some tea, and eat some noodles and fried wheat cakes. Company Commander Bai turned at one point to the leader of the first platoon and said: "There's still one matter left to be resolved. The porcelain bust of the Chairman that we accidentally broke—we can't leave it behind. I'm going to go back and get it."

The platoon leader said, "You're right. But the bust is in pieces. After we bring it back, what will we do with it?"

Without the slightest trace of feeling in his voice or on his face, Bai answered simply, "Let's get it back first and then decide what to do with it. Your men should take care of the students—I'm going to go back alone."

The tall fellow from Shandong Province, his head lowered, obviously downcast, walked over to where Bai was standing and said to him, "I'll go with you."

But Bai didn't utter a word in response to the firm suggestion. He only looked the Shandong guy in the eye, but that serious look in itself was tantamount to rejecting the offer. Turning his head, Bai started off alone with a flashlight in his hand. After a while, Bai returned—empty-handed (save for the flashlight, of course). But there was a look on his face that I had never seen before; it seemed as if he was trying to recover from a shock. In any case, in a dazed tone of voice, he told us, "Something very odd has happened. I looked all over, but there was nothing on the ground to be found." The leader of the first platoon stared in disbelief. "It's impossible. In the small hours of the morning, how could anyone have walked off with it? Did you find the right place?" Bai answered, "Of course I did. If there are any doubts, let's have a small group of men go back and look around. We must find it!" Shortly after this conversation, a few soldiers, including the dejected Shandong fellow and the leader of the first platoon, were chosen to go back and look. I myself proposed going too, saying that as I had been kneeling on a large rock sticking out of the ground—which had caused me great pain—I would surely be able to find the place where we had left the porcelain bust. Actually, I had another purpose in mind: If I did some more walking the wind would dry my pants, which were still wet. At first, the leader of the first platoon was unwilling to let me go along, saying that I looked too tired, but then Bai said, "Since you remember the place, it's best if we let you go back with the others."

Armed with several flashlights, our small band then began to make its way back across the pitch-black open country. We called on our collective memories of our "long march" to lead us back to the small path where we had left the broken pieces of the bust. For my own part, I looked for and eventually found that jagged rock. Drawing on my sense of direction and of distance, I pointed out to the others where the broken pieces lying on the ground should have been. "It's gotta be right here," I said after leading the others to the spot. But what left everyone baffled was that, however we swept our flashlights in wide arcs across the ground, there seemed to be no sign whatsoever of that porcelain bust. Furthermore, even when some of us knelt down to look more carefully, we still could not find even the tiniest bits of porcelain! How bizarre, indeed. Was it possible that someone had come along, picked up the pieces and then taken them away. To do what? And at this odd hour of the night, in this forsaken wilderness; it was scarcely believable. But if so, why had they picked up every single piece, not even leaving the tiniest shard of porcelain behind on the ground?

To the east were fields of sorghum—a flat expanse of inky black stillness, while to the west was a river in which the light from the stars and moon sparkled in silvery enchantment. There was something about the undulations of this reflected light that lulled one into a state of dumbstruck awe that was beyond all comprehension. Looking directly at Commander Bai, I noticed that handsome, pale stern face of his, on which not a trace of feeling was written. Above his lips that mysterious black mole remained stationary.

Still stranger was the fact that after everyone had snapped out of their stupor, we all remained silent and didn't bother to begin looking again. We wound up going straight back to the village. In the schoolhouse, I put three or four desks together to make a bed on which I lay down. But I didn't sleep a wink that night. I couldn't figure out what had really happened. As soon as it was light the next morning, the company set out from the village and thus recommenced our field training. Commander Bai was able to borrow another bust of Chairman Mao from the Military Revolutionary Committee Headquarters. And we got back into waving the red flag, shouting slogans, and singing revolutionary songs—no one mentioned ever again what had happened the previous night.

Perhaps I was too young at the time to unravel the mystery of what took place, let alone understand its significance. I remained bewildered for many years. Then, one day, I suddenly grasped what had happened. The more I thought about it, the more remarkable it seemed to me. And at the same time, I was filled with admiration for the exceptional ability and perspicacity of that taciturn company commander, whom I never saw again. He was the most intelligent man I ever met. From the events that took place, I came away with the following discovery: What is truly clever is not usually recognized as such at the time; it is only much later that one can see and appreciate it for what it was.

In a society that is aberrant, intelligence too grows strange flowers.—F. J.

FOOTNOTE

1. A flat, sesame-seed cake commonly eaten in Northern China.

THE SCIENTIST WHO PIONEERED THE ATOM BOMB

TIME: *1968* 🦋 AGE: *37* 🦋 SEX: *Male*
OCCUPATION: *Former department head at a nuclear research institute in Q province*

I have only one request to make: Please don't treat the experiences I'm about to describe to you as material for a "freak story." I don't want to let others make use of the bumpy, tortuous road I have followed just to satisfy their curiosity. I hope instead that by telling my story, I'll enable them to get a glimpse into the core of the experiences I've lived through. My sufferings aren't merely personal, they also represent to a large extent the turmoil that a generation of intellectuals went through.

Let me state first that the production of an atom bomb was not the mysterious process some people imagine it to be. Nor was it the result of the best scientists locking themselves up in a laboratory for days and then coming up with some miracle. Of course, I admit it is necessary to have scientists provide a theoretical basis for these breakthroughs as well as draw up plans for their realization. But in order for their discoveries to be brought to the light of day and put to use in production, it is imperative that the project begin with the basics, with meticulous attention paid to operations, trial runs, observations, and the like. This huge endeavor requires the intelligence, perseverance, dexterity, and hard work of thousands of intellectuals, technicians, soldiers, and administrative personnel. I have been just one person in the ranks of the people involved, albeit at the front lines. My mission—and that of others like myself—has been to tackle the first set of problems, research, and experimentation.

I come from an educated family. My grandfather was a teacher during the late Qing dynasty. Although my family is from Wuxi, I grew up not far away from Shanghai. When I was in high school, before Liberation, I participated in the underground Communist Party movement. As my past history and background were known to be free of problems, I was able to move up within the Party organization to positions of considerable responsibility. After Liberation, I attended Qinghua University in Beijing. When I graduated, I was sent to the Soviet Union for advanced studies. I won't talk about my formal, technical training because the subject really is too complex and because it would thus be too difficult for you to write down clearly. I'll only talk about the events that took place around me.

When I returned to China in 1960, the Party organization told me that they wanted me to work on a matter of the utmost importance related to national defense. It turned out to be a research project on the atom bomb. Earlier, we had placed our hopes in the belief that the Soviet Union would offer us technical assistance in this endeavor, but in 1959, these hopes were dashed because of the break in Sino-Soviet relations. Instead, we decided to try to develop an atom bomb by ourselves. But in our case, this was easier said than done, as we lacked the solid technical foundation that would have enabled us to carry out such work smoothly, especially since it involved such an advanced area of science. The difficult task of developing an atom bomb for China was entrusted to research institute No. 9 of the Nuclear Industry Ministry. The mission itself was top secret at the time; within the ministry itself, it was referred to by the code number 596.

In June 1959, preliminary work on the first atom bomb began. At that time, I was one of only a handful of research workers less than thirty years old, all of whom had been through a rigorous selection process and had the complete trust of the Party organization. Naturally, I felt honored. Furthermore, I became the envy of a lot of intellectuals, what with my impeccable personal history, spotless family background, and of course, my having been selected to work on the first atom bomb in China. Moreover, I had no impediments in my way, and no real worries about my job or future.

Nonetheless, when I first arrived at the research base, what impressed me the most was the complete desolateness of the terrain. It was in a barren, sandy part of Qinghai Province in Northwest China, really a dreary, difficult place to live and work! This area had originally been used by Tibetans as a yak grazing area, so there was only grass as far as the eye could see. During the course of a year, one would become aware, too, of the elements—the sun, the moon, the strong winds, the scorching heat, the bitter cold—that made up this solitary universe. Now that I think of it, there were wolves too.

From our own viewpoint, we were like the first settlers there. At the beginning, we lived in tents. Sleeping in them at night, we could hear the wind rushing about and the wolves howling. Due to the high altitude—we were about 3,000 meters above sea level—our chests felt as if they were filled with sand and our throats as if they had been plugged up with stoppers. Furthermore, for the same reason, it was difficult for us to steam our *mantou*.[1]

About this time as well, China was going through a difficult period,[2] in which transportation was disrupted, and as we were not given special consideration of any sort, we were seriously short of scientific instruments and materials. Nonetheless, we were still filled with a kind of heroic enthusiasm, believing as we did that we had to prove ourselves and that we had to produce China's first atom bomb no matter what. I was very fond of repeating to myself a term used in physics, "aerodynamics," which describes the forces applied by moving air on objects, to remind myself that the burning enthusiasm we were filled with was a motive force that once ignited would enable us to overcome any and all obstacles. Although we were standing out there in the middle of nothing with our hands empty and with not even a single spare part with which to build an atom bomb, this burning drive could be harnessed to work for us, to move us forward. We were willing to give our lives to fulfill the mission our country had entrusted us with. The new generation of young people today may ridicule us for being "the devoted, or docile," generation, but it is true nonetheless that at the time we felt a great deal of personal fulfillment in our work!

Thus, as soon as we arrived, we threw ourselves at once into the intense work we had before us. The most important thing at the beginning was to do a pilot experiment under simulated conditions with nonnuclear materials. We would be watching for the manifestation of certain properties and principles as well as to see whether they conformed to our own indicators. The rest of our work was similar in format—to see whether or not the results of our experimentation conformed with the parameters of our original plan. I was responsible for calculating all the measurements and was the head of a group of researchers entrusted with this task. A great deal was riding on it because each major experiment was extremely costly. If we had been unable to obtain the data we needed, the whole effort would have been a total waste. As our collective sense of responsibility and of the importance of such experimentation was very high, we had to be extremely meticulous in every aspect of our work. Not only that, we also had to be totally concentrated on what we were doing. It would not be false to say that we considered the mission of producing China's first atom bomb even more important than our own lives.

One of the main reasons we were able to achieve success in the experimental phase of our work on the atom bomb within such a short period of time was that we had taken painstaking efforts to ensure the soundness of our foundations.

With our small experimental model as a "preview," toward the end of 1963 we were able to successfully complete all work related to this phase of our mission. In 1964, we gave the small experimental model another test, and in April and May of that same year we were able to conduct a test of a larger model, one comparable in dimensions to the actual bomb that was to be produced. The only difference was that we used TNT instead of fissionable materials. This phase of our project was extremely important, as its successful completion was essential to the nuclear experimentation that followed.

During this time we were living in a compound off the base. For several consecutive days and nights—with no break in between—we took the utmost care to make sure that every-

thing was working the way it was supposed to. The results of
the test with the larger model were a stupendous success. Taking the data plus the photographic negatives with me, I rushed
over to the main compound where I processed the negatives
and developed the prints. How eager I was to go over to the
command headquarters and tell them of the news! When I got
there, the higher-ups who were all waiting there included the
headquarters chief, comrade Li Jue, as well as responsible parties from Beijing. When I rushed into the room, there was a
moment of complete silence, and all eyes in the room turned
toward me. I told them, "It was a success!" and then gave them
the photographs to show them. Everyone was ecstatic; they
saluted each other, embraced, drank liquor, and sang songs.
Comrade Li smiled a wide grin and told me to go and quickly
get some sleep. But for some reason, my eyelids, which had been
fighting the past few days and nights to stay open, suddenly
would not shut; lying down on the bed, I just could not get to
sleep. I was probably overexcited. But when I finally did manage to slip into a doze, I slept for one whole day. Since I had
arrived in the grasslands of Qinghai Province, I had never slept
so well. Although when I sleep I almost always have dreams,
this time I didn't dream at all. Moreover, the fatigue I had been
storing up over so many days and nights was finally lifted clean
from me.

In this way, we were able to proceed to the last phase of the
mission: to test a real atom bomb. In July and August of 1964,
the hottest time of the year, we carried a complete set of measuring instruments to a region of the Gobi Desert where the
sparse vegetation was so baked by the sun that not one drop of
water could be seen on it and where the birds themselves were
so hot that they could not fly. In spite of this, a steel tower had
been erected there to serve as the launching pad. We assembled

our instruments on it, and then we also installed other equipment at the No. 5 detonation site, which was not far from the control tower. The two groups of equipment were connected by wiring. Once the nuclear explosion took place the wiring would snap at the same time as the instruments on the launching pad would completely explode. The most valuable data would all be safely stored in the equipment at the second location. In the unlikely event that the equipment and instruments failed to function properly, God only knew whether the explosion would be successful or not. Furthermore, such a malfunction would entail an enormous economic cost as well as a tremendous waste of hours. I felt a huge amount of responsibility weighing on my own shoulders. The walls of the No. 5 detonation site were made of a particularly solid kind of cement, one that would not be destroyed in an explosion. During the day, the temperatures would be excruciatingly high, while at night they would drop to bitter lows. Sleep? Those next days we practically forgot who we were, caught up as we were in our work. Figuratively speaking, we became our instruments; our minds were totally fixed on the atom bomb and on nothing else.

Chief commanding officer Li came to the nuclear experimental base, too, several times. A former army general who had assisted in the liberation of Tibet, Li knew practically nothing about nuclear technology. But he had the upright, distinguished bearing of his former vocation. When we had first arrived in Qinghai, we had lived with him in a tent. Later, when buildings had been put up to house base personnel, we moved into them. But he insisted on continuing to live in the tent, saying that we deserved to live in better quarters. What a contrast with the leaders of work units in China today!

By October 15, everything was ready for our first real explosion. All the equipment had been installed and set up. At this time, we began to evacuate, moving to a radiation-free area fifty or so kilometers away. Commander Li was the last to leave the launching site because someone had to climb up the steel tower to install the detonator, since at that point the elevators were not working because there was no electricity. Although the detonator had been checked many times before, we would be facing disaster if by chance it slipped while we were preparing to install it. Moreover, after it had been properly installed, the person who had climbed up would still have to climb down. Concerned and vigilant, Li waited for him at the bottom of the steel tower. Later, from fifty kilometers away, I gave Li a telephone call to see if everything was all right. He was still at the site, stubborn and heroic. Such was the overall caliber of the team of scientists, cadres, technicians, and backup staff working on this pioneering mission.

At last, we waited for the command to come from the central government. When we were notified by Beijing, the countdown began: ten, nine, eight, . . . two, one, and zero! But in that last second there was no sign of any explosion. We were paralyzed with anxiety, our hearts almost stopped, and out throats constricted. Did it fail? If it did, that might mean we would have to start all over again from scratch. But actually, only a few seconds after the zero call, fifty or sixty kilometers from the site of the explosion, we suddenly saw a gigantic mushroomlike cloud of smoke appear and begin to rise slowly up in the air. Stunned, we began to jump up and down, shout, and scream until our throats were hoarse, Some people were so excited that they jumped up into the air and landed on their rear ends afterward, but they didn't care! This was China's first atom bomb and it had been successful! And it was we who had been responsible for it, who had brought it forth from nothing with our bare hands! But if you had been on the scene and had worked on the same mission, you would have felt that our success was far from merely a festive occasion, for that great billowing mushroom cloud that had risen in the northwest was the product of the sweat, tears, and brains of thousands of people who gave of themselves so wholeheartedly over the space of so many years. No one had participated in it out of a concern for financial gain. As I had personally taken part in the mission, I had come into contact with countless numbers of heroic people whose names I never knew—researchers, highly skilled technicians, administrators, as well as those involved in refining, concentration, or processing substances—all these people had given of themselves with no thought of gaining anything financial in return. Before I forget it, there were also the antichemical warfare corps who, after the explosion, had to rush to the actual site and bring back certain substances that would aid us in determining the actual effectiveness of the explosion. The protective uniforms they wore must have been drenched with sweat.

Before the Cultural Revolution, the nuclear base in Qinghai Province had grown into a small city, with its own department store, movie theater, hospital, and schools. In short, it had everything a city of its size needed. All of us there felt plenty of confidence in the future and in the work we were doing. At the same time, all of us still had a great many tasks lying before us. Before the first nuclear explosion, I had married a woman who had come to Xinjiang without the slightest hesitation, so we had both left everything behind to live entirely for the life we were to lead here.

But the coming of the Cultural Revolution was like a man-made political atom bomb that was thrown onto our base.

Everything was turned upside down. Even though we had developed the hydrogen bomb by the end of 1967, most of the essential work leading up to the final explosion had been done before the Cultural Revolution.

During the Cultural Revolution, rumors circulated on the outside that I had been executed in front of a firing squad or that I had committed suicide. During the period when we were working on the hydrogen bomb, I was still the head of a research department with a total staff of over 100. People have asked me before, did the Cultural Revolution also take place where we scientists had been working to develop the first atom bomb in China? A rather obvious question—for wasn't it said at the time that wherever there were two people, there were bound to be two factions locked in fierce struggle? Every struggle at that time was ruthless and violent. Our base was divided into two opposing factions, one of which was supported by the People's Liberation Army (which entered at one point into the conflict) and the other which the army tried to nail. Needless to say, the participation of the army in the conflict increased the violence. One faction was called the Grasslands Red Guards and the other the August First Red Guards.[3] But it was often unclear who was attacking whom. For our part, after 1968, we intellectuals tried to stay out of the conflict and remain neutral. But most intellectuals had at least some problem connected with their backgrounds, and even if they hadn't, someone was bound to concoct one for them. In my particular case, I was branded with "four points," which were antithetical with the Four Cardinal Points (Principles) enunciated by Lin Biao. As to their exact content and order, I really can't remember anymore, but they seemed to go as follows: my "get the job done first" versus Lin Biao's "make politics number one"; my "work performance foremost" versus Lin Biao's "ideological thinking is paramount" and so on. (It has always been difficult for me to remember them.) The charges brought against me as a result of these four diametrically opposed pairs of views led to my house being ransacked—the cabinets, drawers, and boxes being overturned and rummaged through. My wife was in a state of flustered anxiety when this happened—she was a nursery school teacher, an honest person who was afraid of trouble, fearing as she did that something was going to happen to me. But I thought to myself that the whole thing would run its course and then that would be that. After all, my family background was spotless: As a youth, I had joined the underground party and further-more, I was only in charge of a research body and had been uninvolved in the factional strife all along, having said little if anything about the goings-on. So what could possibly happen to me? I thought to myself. As one involved in developing the atom bomb, even if it could not be said that I had an achieve-ment to my name, at the very least it had to be admitted that I had worked hard and doggedly. Surely even an insub-stantial contribution could not be confused with committing a bad act.

I had no idea at all that the unforeseen would happen. In 1969, things around here were in a complete state of chaos: Most of the staff was doing nothing in terms of professional work. All that they did was engage in interfactional feuding or write big-character poster denouncing so-and-so. At that time, Li, who had been the overall director of the base, came under heavy attack, and all experimental testing had stopped. In our confusion and uncertainty, we still believed that we would weather the storm and then resume our work. But we kept waiting and waiting...one day suddenly the directive came from higher up announcing that the scope of our research activ-ities had been too wide and that, with the imminent possibility of an air attack from the Soviet revisionists, we would have to move inland. So everything had to be packed into chests and boxes. Refused permission to leave, some of us, myself included, had to remain at the main compound, while the branch unit moved inland. In retrospect, I think it must have been some workers who were hoping to pilfer a few things who pried open the drawers of my desk in my old office and made off with a very top secret work manual.

It was at this point that my luck turned sour. Someone reported the loss of that manual to the authorities in Beijing, who promptly sent over two high-ranking officials to investigate. One of them was the second-in-command of the Ministry of Public Security, the other a senior naval officer. Both of them were bent on kicking up a lot of dust, so they mounted a vigorous campaign to blow up the incident of the missing top secret work manual into evidence supporting their theory that in our work unit there were people trying to pull the system down and take the capitalist road. In this way, the whole country would be rocked by the "revelations" of a "conspiracy." And the reverberations of the shock, they believed, would propel the Cultural Revolution forward into a new, even more convulsive phase, one that would totally negate the past. As both of these men were referred to as "senior Central Committee leaders," they were armed with considerable political clout and prestige, which they used to declare with absolute certainty that counter-revolutionary agents had stolen that work manual of mine. Then they moved quickly to seize people and have them summarily executed in front of a firing squad.

Thus, a reign of terror began in which some people were killed, others committed suicide, the killers were labeled "counterrevolutionary agents," and then in turn were seized and executed as well. Many innocent people were rounded up and persecuted. Things reached a crescendo of disorder, and even the trains stopped running through here. It seemed as though the grasslands themselves had returned to a state of primeval violence and barbarity.

In our own research section, someone was apprehended who had had no problems before but who, when he returned to his hometown of Changsha in Hunan Province, had bumped into a relative from Hong Kong who was visiting his family. Here was proof! Without a shadow of a doubt, a spy! The two "senior Central Committee leaders," bringing a party of their followers, intervened after they learned of this last incident. Using a variety of coercive measures, they made the man confess to having set up a counterrevolutionary espionage network as well as a secret code. First, the man was beaten into a sorry state, and then he and his wife were interrogated separately and forced to write statements about what mistakes they had made in the past, and the two statements were compared to see if there were any discrepancies. The rounds of forced confessions and beatings nearly did them both in. At one point, the man, unable to bear any more, began to wildly throw accusations about, incriminating me and a few others. So now I was brought into it! It became "known" that he and I had gotten together to steal top secret government documents. Furthermore, they could hardly let me go scot-free as I was the "ring-leader" and he only my lackey! In the aftermath of this revelation, I was locked up in what had before been a laboratory and became for a time a "laboratory specimen." Outside the door were several PLA guards, who could peer inside to observe my actions through a hole that had been bored in the door. I was perhaps more like at atom bomb or some other deadly secret chemical that had to be zealously guarded at all times than simply a lab specimen! At the beginning of my incarceration, I could not really believe that all this was happening to me, thinking all the while about how as a young man I had joined the underground party, how in my middle years I had worked on China's first atom bomb, been considered a veteran revolutionary . . . Premier Zhou Enlai had even once received me. Dwelling on the past, I thought to myself, "When I met with Premier Zhou, Lin Biao was there. . . . I talked with them both."

But the Cultural Revolution had to sweep away everything . . . the past was of no consequence. Even founding fathers of the revolution had to bite the dust and lower their heads. Who was I? You were just what they told you you were! As things went on, the ranks of the counterrevolutionary spies that had been rooted out multiplied. And the laboratory where I was locked up filled up with other prisoners, sleeping two to a bed. Thus, I began to see that there was not much hope. During the daytime, each of us prisoners had to sit on a small stool reading the *Quotations of Chairman Mao*, reflecting on our "bad ways," undergoing interrogation, and explaining our past behavior. None of us dared to talk to the others. It wasn't until 2:00 A.M. that we were allowed to sleep a while and even then we couldn't put out the lights, as they were afraid we might commit suicide. But try as they did to get me to confess, I would not fabricate stories incriminating myself or other people. This elicited charges that I was still fighting stubbornly with my back to the wall and that I was the most recalcitrant of the whole lot of prisoners. So the consensus was that they would have to use still more severe tactics on me and begin new rounds of struggle in order to get me to confess.

One day, a group of people were supposed to be shot in front of a firing squad. I recall that among the people about to be executed, there was a surgeon at the base who had once during an operation accidentally made a small mistake. Under ordinary circumstances, this would not have been considered anything other than a minor accident. But now it was blown up into a serious matter, for the surgeon was considered a member of the class of capitalist-intellectuals, while the patient was a People's Liberation Army soldier and a stalwart pillar of the dictatorship of the proletariat. The situation was a powder keg of sorts, if you wanted to look at it that way. In any case, the accident smacked of class revenge and this in itself demanded a repayment in blood. So, the surgeon was to be taken out and shot.

Then there was the case of the recent college graduate, who, like everyone else in his boat, had a low monthly stipend to live on. This fellow, it has to be said, was not of the best fiber—in terms of morale and discipline, at least—and he got to complaining. "If my stipend isn't raised, I'm going to go and wreck the detonator!" he murmured under his breath one day. But no sooner had the words escaped his mouth than people latched onto them and exposed him, saying that here indeed was another bona fide counterrevolutionary spy just waiting to cause trouble! Although he had spoken those really inappropriate words practically in an aside to himself and in no case would have really gone and done such a thing, people said that "after all, no one forced him to say it—he said it himself!" So he, too, was charged with being an active counterrevolutionary and to be executed in front of a firing squad.

Finally, the day came when a huge mass meeting was held during which a number of people, including myself, were to be executed. The atmosphere was filled with terror, and the masses were waiting in tense anticipation. Rumor had it that even within the ranks of the masses, there were a number of counterrevolutionary spies as well as other potentially suspect individuals as well. No one knew who might be dragged out and shot to death right on the spot.

A group of us were tied up and escorted to the execution ground, where we were forced to line up in front of the podium. I had no illusions—I thought I knew very well what was going to happen, and so my mind was actually blank. To tell the truth, I was in such a stupor that my thoughts were not even on my wife, whom, if I was going to die, I would never see again. My mind was racing above the clouds, oblivious to the actual moment. In the meantime, one by one, people's names were called out, their crime spelled out, and the final punishment—in each case, execution in front of a firing squad—announced. But when the last name on the list was read, my name had still not been called out! It was at this point that I grew conscious of my existence and became aware that I was actually standing there with both feet on the ground. The others —including the surgeon and the recent college graduate—had all been taken somewhere not far off to be executed. And the sounds of guns being fired were distinct and resonant . . . all of those people fell by the wayside. After the firing had stopped, members of the "tribunal" said to me, "Did you hear those shots? If you don't start telling the truth, tomorrow it'll be you!" Then they began to attack me, mostly verbally. Out of a desire to amply show their revolutionary spirit as well as out of a fear of being executed themselves, the crowd around me began to shout verbal abuse at me with a particularly vociferous ferocity.

Had I really luckily escaped from the clutches of death? Later, I learned that the real reason for my not having been executed was that the "tribunal" believed that I was a "ringleader" of a counterrevolutionary clique that was intent on stealing national secrets; if I were executed right away, it would hinder efforts to track the whereabouts, identity and convoluted criminal activities of my other accomplices, who were believed to be numerous.

The executions, and their talk about them, had been used simply to scare the wits out of me. Nonetheless, the last round of executions left me with the deep, painful realization that life can indeed be taken away very easily.

The reign of terror lasted for a long while afterward, with a number of alleged "counterrevolutionary spies" still being arrested. Some of these persecuted people tried to run away, but their efforts were mostly in vain, because all around the research base was nothing but empty, seemingly infinite grasslands. If some people did manage to escape, the army would be sure to pursue them, and when they were caught and brought back, they would be even more cruelly abused and beaten. One ex-soldier who had tried to run away was beaten so savagely that he picked up a spade and furiously tried to defend himself. Of course, he failed to ward off his tormentors and was executed shortly after. But as the number of people identified and persecuted as counterrevolutionary spies began to swell, the focus of attention also began to shift from myself to other more important "targets." In fact, the most recently discovered "counterrevolutionaries" always became the objects of the most intense scrutiny and attack. When the heat was off me, I had a chance to escape into the recesses of my mind and think about my own scientific interests. Even though my career was over and I didn't have the slightest hope left, for a time I entertained myself by thinking about my work. The fact that I did so perhaps reflects the bookworm-ish tendencies that all intellectuals share. And it's also possible that somewhere in my unconscious I actually did harbor some hope of being able one day to continue doing my work. I began to think about my wife, the only person I really missed. I wondered to myself: Where is she? What is she doing? I had no idea about what might have happened to her. I hated myself, thinking that I had brought harm to her.

Some years later, when the nuclear research base institute moved east, I was put on a freight train carrying coal and sent to a valley nestled in the mountains somewhere in Sichuan Province, where I continued to be persecuted and undergo heavy criticism.

It was not until Lin Biao fell from power that things took a turn for the better for my hapless self. I was able to return to Beijing, to my wife's great shock—she never thought I would appear on her doorstep one day. At any rate, it seemed like we could never finish telling each other all about the things that had happened to us over the years of our separation. Later, too, a research institute in Beijing became interested in hiring me, which I agreed to. It was only from this time on that I was able to gradually put the past—all the vicissitudes, unhappiness, suffering, fleeting glory—behind me.

I heard that when Director Li had found out that I had been forced to leave the nuclear research institute, he was not happy about it. But at this point, he himself was no longer in a position of top-level responsibility, although he still wished to do something for the country, thinking, as he often did, about how for a time in the past we had rocked the country with our pluck, intelligence, sweat, dogged determination. But didn't I have the same feeling, too . . . ?

If there was anything in the world more terrifying in its impact than the atom bomb, it must have been the Cultural Revolution.

Really the only aspiration that intellectuals in China have is to be able to accomplish something, to be able to work in peace. But because of this desire, they have suffered calamity—this is what gives them the greatest pain. Bearing their suffering patiently, they still aspire to do something for their country. So, would you say that this aspiration, this thirst for knowledge, is their strong point or their fatal flaw? Nowadays, there are some people who say it's their outstanding attribute. Is this true? I leave this question open for you to probe—after all, you are a writer. We scientists have never really understood the nature of our dilemma all along.

Looking back on the fates of my colleagues at the nuclear research base, I can state that each of them had an individual path laid out for him, though each path was in varying degrees rocky and arduous.

Of course, there were a few people who, shrilly shouting the slogans of the time and fanning the flames, jumped on Chairman Mao's bandwagon to become the lieutenants of the late leader's "thought corps." These same individuals saw their careers skyrocket for a while, but whether they had a nice landing later on remained to be seen.

Then there were people who suffered more than I did—for instance, a scientist who was forced by the soldiers who surrounded him to run all day around the inside of the compound shouting, "Leniency to those who confess their crimes and severity to those who refuse!" and "Those who are incorrigible in the end choose death."

For my part, I have nothing to be ashamed of—I didn't harm anyone, so my conscience is clean. I did a few good things, so I didn't let down either the Party or the people. I have kept to one principle all along: to have honest dealings with others, to be steadfast in my work. Though I suffered greatly through the Cultural Revolution, what happened to me is over forever. Whatever my country asks me to do, I am still willing to work hard to accomplish. All my country has to do is call me.

*The tragedy of the yellow earth—suffering the winds of change
yet still caring and bearing fruit.*—F. J.

FOOTNOTES

1. A kind of leavened dough eaten in Northern China.

2. The Great Leap Forward was in full swing, with millions of
people dying of malnutrition.

3. August first is the anniversary of the founding of the People's
Liberation Army.

health care:
"bad elements," care denied
to, 44
in countryside, 21–22, 138–
39
doctors' experiences, 51–52
mistreatment of patients, 44–
45
in prison, 47–48
Hou Jun, 64
housing conditions, 33
Hua Guofeng, 139, 145n6
Hu Yaobang, 145n6

ideology meetings, 78
ideology reform programs for
students, 95–97
informers, 57
career advancement by, 34–
36
motivations of, 31–32

Jian Bozan, 71
Jiang Qing, 37n2, 91
Red Guard, meetings with,
84–85
Jia Zhi, 85

Kuomintang (KMT), 27n18

letters:
from children to parents, 9–11
from prisoners to families,
116–17, 118–21

Liberation from Japan, 4
libraries, closing of, 200
Li Jue, 229, 230, 231, 234, 241
Lin Biao, 84, 103n18, 233, 237,
241
"Little Red Book," 47, 53n2
Liu Shaoqi, 102n15
Long March, 51, 54n4
Luo Longji, 145n2
Lu Xun, 81, 102n14

Mao Dun, 85, 103n19
"Mao hiding in a ditch" story,
search for, 198–206
Mao Zedong:
on "four existences," 10
idolization of, 86
Red Guard, criticism of, 93
Red Guard, meetings with,
82–84
on right to rebel, 72
Mao Zedong Thought
Workers' Propaganda
Team, 92, 104n28
marriage as means to social
acceptability, 165–67
"marriage decision" incident,
172–77
mentally ill, mistreatment of,
60
Military Control Commission,
45, 53n1
military training for general
population, 210

struggle sessions, 6, 26*n*9, 134
  children subjected to, 188–89
suicide attempts:
  capitalists, 41–44
  "monsters," 133
  prison inmates, 202–3
  punishment for, 45–46
  rape victims, 13
  reactionaries, 73
  relatives of Rightists, 134–35
  torture victims, 31, 32
  wives of
    counterrevolutionaries,
    117

Tao Zhu, 82, 102*n*15
teaching positions, 163
Tian Han, 85, 103*n*21
TV college, 24, 27*n*26
"two-line struggle," 10, 27*n*16

Wang Hongwen, 37*n*2
Wang Jie, 68
Water Margin (novel), 196
wheat gathering, 67
wives of
  counterrevolutionaries,
  105–6

childrearing, 111–12, 114
divorce forced upon, 110–11,
  115–17
husbands' letters to, 116–17,
  118–21
suicide attempts, 117
supporting the family, 112
visits to imprisoned
  husbands, 109–10, 112–
  13
women, revolutionary, 95
writers, denunciations of, 85–
  86

Xie Juezai, 205
Xing Yangzhi, 64

Yao Wenyuan, 37*n*2, 120,
  127*n*1
Youth League, 15, 27*n*20

Zhang Bojun, 145*n*2
Zhang Qunqiao, 37*n*2
Zhang Xianliang, 101*n*2
Zhang Yonglin, 65, 101*n*2
Zhao Ziyang, 145*n*6
Zhou Enlai, 237

ABOUT THE AUTHOR

Feng Jicai is one of China's leading contemporary writers of both fiction and nonfiction. He is author of *Chrysanthemum and Other Stories*, among other books.